WOVEN STORIES

WOVEN STORIES

Andean Textiles and Rituals

ANDREA M. HECKMAN

UNIVERSITY OF NEW MEXICO PRESS ■ ALBUQUERQUE

This book is dedicated to

the memory of Alfonso Ortiz,

teacher, scholar, storyteller,

and friend

LIBRARY OF CONGRESS CATALOGING-IN-PUBLICATION DATA

Heckman, Andrea M., 1947—
    Woven stories : Andean textiles and rituals / Andrea M. Heckman.— 1st ed.
        p.   cm.
    Includes bibliographical references and index.
    ISBN 0-8263-2934-9 (cloth : alk. paper)
1. Quechua textile fabrics—Peru—Pacchanta. 2. Quechua weavers—Peru—Pacchanta.
3. Quechua women—Peru—Pacchanta—Rites and ceremonies.
4. Hand weaving—Peru—Pacchanta—Patterns.
5. Pacchanta (Peru)--Social life and customs. I. Title.
    F2230.2.K4 H43 2003
    746.1′4′08998323085—dc21

                                                                    2002008809

BOOK DESIGN AND COMPOSITION BY MINA YAMASHITA
PRINTED AND BOUND BY SUNG IN PRINTING KOREA, LTD.

Always tell a story from the beginning

Telling a story from the beginning is re-knowing the experience.

This is the way all things have always been.

That's what the Pueblo elders say.

—Chino et al., Surviving Columbus (1992)

When you experience something

It becomes more and more deeply rooted in you

And you change, you transform.

Make your practice alive, experiential, and deep.

—Zhang Zhung Nyam Gyu

CONTENTS

FOREWORD

Garth Bawden

This is a remarkable book about textiles and their meaning to the lives of their makers—the *runakuna,* Quechua speakers of Ausangate and neighboring communities of the remote highlands of southern Peru. Dr. Andrea Heckman brings to these pages an unusual level of experience, acquired from decades of travel in the Andes. More important, she has shared the lives of the villagers, and as an accomplished weaver herself, has used her art and its craft as the means to surmount the distance that usually persists between even the most sensitive anthropological scholars and the subjects of their observation. However, the book acquires its exceptional quality because of the relationship to the weavers and their families that the author brings to her writing. She not only brings the knowledge of an accomplished academic to her work, impressive though this is, but also the understanding of one who has lived with these people, speaks their language, and has been accepted into their lives and culture to an extent that has rarely been matched. By living for long periods of time in the highland villages, she has become a member of their social lives. Her several local godchildren and her position as a ritual sponsor (*cargo* holder) in the village of Ollantaytambo has given her a level of respect and responsibility in the social and ritual life of the area that is hard to appreciate by reference to modern North America where such roles are becoming increasingly honorary.

The thesis of this book is that the weavers of Ausangate and their highland counterparts encode the cultural beliefs that support their individual and community identity in the complex designs of their textiles. Weaving plays an important role in daily life by materializing the relationships between living and ancestral members of these communities, accentuating their fundamental connection to community land and its sacred places, and evoking the rituals through which they continually vitalize their enduring traditions. To a greater extent than any other writer, Andrea Heckman's acceptance into the daily lives of the people of Ausangate has given her deep insight into the impact of Western modernity on the traditional culture of the Andean highlands. Her experience shows that the often reiterated view that the intrusion of the modern Western world with its commercial values and commodities signals the end of traditional Andean culture is simplistic and largely inaccurate. In fact, foreign innovations resulting from this cultural interaction, such as the increasing adoption of synthetic yarns for weaving, are utilized within the framework of existing cosmology where they become useful tools for propagating traditional practices and concepts.

On a broader level, this book highlights the universal human capacity to transcend the challenges of history and to sustain the authoritative legacy of traditional understanding in the face of innovation and change. From her deep love and admiration for the people about which she writes, sentiments richly reciprocated by them, the author brings us a tribute to the tenacity and creativity of the human spirit that is rarely seen in anthropological literature.

ACKNOWLEDGMENTS

My deepest thanks are sent on a prayer back to Ausangate, to her people, her land, and her presence, truly one of the world's great mountains. Don Mariano Turpo blessed this study from the beginning; Juan Victor Núñez del Prado helped me find all that I was searching for; and Jorge Flores Ochoa, with his ever-gracious manner, was a helpful influence on this research. The unknowing heroes are, of course, Maria Merma Gonzalo, friend and primary weaving teacher; her mother Manuela and all their family members, including distant aunts in Upis; Maria's son Eloy and his wife, Verjidia; his brother Eusavio and his new wife; and especially Silea, Maria's only daughter, who accompanied me up the mountain to Mariano's place and spun yarn with me. I am also thankful to my compadres, godchildren, and friends in Pacchanta, Ninaparayoq, Uchuy Finaya, Puka Qocha, Upis, and Tinqi, as well as Ollantaytambo and Cuzco. Luis Pacsi and Mario Turpo are responsible for my understanding of *qocha*s. Timoteo CCarita and his wife Benita from Pitumarka are the real weaving and dye experts. Special thanks to all who have helped, especially Gloria Tamayo, Luis Morató Peña, and Garland Bills, my patient Quechua teachers; Wendy Weeks and Robert, Nathan and Joaquin Randall of Ollantaytambo, and Peter Frost of Cuzco.

Immeasurable thanks are due to many people at the University of New Mexico, including Garth Bawden, an associate, friend, and co-trip leader; Flora Clancy, Mari Lyn Salvador, Ed Lieuwen, Joanie Swanson, Gil Merkx, and especially the late Alfonso Ortiz.

Grants made the many years of this research possible, including the Tinker Foundation (1982), Carnegie-Mellon Foundation (1983), Foreign Language Advanced Studies (FLAS, U.S. government Title VI, 1994), Fulbright Foundation (1996), and the Latin American Institute at the University of New Mexico for fieldwork funding. Catherine Allen, Anthony Aveni, Joseph Bastien, Richard Burger, Rosie Blum, Nilda Callañaupa, Ann Rowe, and Elayne Zorn, have all been friends, lending me kind ears and good company. Special thanks goes to Catherine Baudoin and Ian Wagoner at the

Maxwell Museum. Thanks to Pat Pollard and Ed Ranney for help with the selection of photos.

Bill Abbott, owner of Wilderness Travel, has sent me to far corners of the earth with friendship and good humor. Thanks to Ray Rodney, Julie Wilson, Barbara Banks, Kim Thomas, Melanie Safford, Heather Navarre, Barbara Wright, Gretchen Bains, Caryn Dombrowski, and Monica Cable, all hard-working staff and supporters at Wilderness Travel. Thanks to Sandra Ratto Risso and her husband Felix and Ricky Schiller in Lima, and to Maria del Carmen in Cuzco, and all the staff of Chasquitur, including local guides, Kika Caballero, Diana Hidalgo, and Marco Aragon.

Thanks to Rosie Braun, Deborah Bernal, Terry Davis, and Terry Petree for tending the home fires for all the years that I was in Peru. I have the greatest appreciation and thanks to my parents, Andy and Margaret Anderson, and my brother Mike Anderson for their confidence and support for so many years. It is hard to express enough thanks to my husband, Ken O'Neil, who met me in Peru and has understood with great patience and support this life that I lead.

Thanks finally to Luther Wilson, director; David Holtby, editor-in-chief; Mina Yamashita, designer extraordinaire; and staff at the University of New Mexico Press for help in all aspects of publishing this book. I am deeply indebted to the friends who have traveled to Peru with me over the last twenty-two years who had faith in this book and in me to give donations to the University of New Mexico Foundation in support of this book, which made the color reproductions possible.

Contributors

Charles and Edythe Anderson, Taos, New Mexico

Judith Anderson, Phoenix, Arizona

The Agans, Granville, Ohio

Art and Susan Bachrach, Taos, New Mexico

Maurice and Lillian Barbash, Brightwaters, New York

Dr. Mujeebunisa Baig, Warren, Ohio

Andrezej and Joanna Borowiec, Chicago, Illinois

Lewis Bowers, Springfield, Oregon

Neil and Linda Brownstein, Palo Alto, California

Jim and Mary Burns, Taos, New Mexico

Susan Compernolle, Chicago, Illinois

Peter and Linda M. de Leon, Denver, Colorado

Richard and Sheila Duffy, Wellfleet, Massachusetts

Dr. Robert and Reta Fitch, Taos, New Mexico

David Hughes and Sharon McGill, La Jolla, California

Keith and Catherine Hughes, Cambridge, Massachusetts

Frank and Connie Houde, Albany, New York

Norman Fritz, Mill Valley, California

John and Nancy Glasgow, El Prado, New Mexico

Susan Glenn, Blowing Rock, North Carolina

Rick and Pam Johnsen, Issaquah, Washington

Jane A. Kennedy, Portland, Oregon

K. Stan and Kathy Martin, Lake Oswego, Oregon

Dr. Marvin and Diane Miller, Elm Grove, Wisconsin

Joan Monego, Elmwood Park, Illinois

Ralph Myers and Jody Zamora-Myers,
    Carmel Valley, California

Bruce Norman, Taos, New Mexico

Norman Pickell, Torrance, California

Wesley and Jean Pittman, Taos, New Mexico

Phyllis Ransopher-Nottingham, Dallas, Texas

Margaret Polly Raye, Taos, New Mexico

Rick and Jean Richards, Taos, New Mexico

Scott and Karen Rogers, Albuquerque, New Mexico

Isabel Schmidt, Naramata, British Columbia, Canada

David and Patricia Smail, Fairfax, Virginia

Dr. Susan Sneider, Burnsville, North Carolina

McHenry and Anne Stiff III, Round Hill, Virginia

John and Carol Sykora, Seal Beach, California

Syd Teague, Austin, Texas

Bruce and Ivy Weiss, Key West, Florida

Jim and Nan Youngerman, Madison, Wisconsin

Cynthia E. Wilson, San Francisco, California

Rugged peaks of the Cordillera Huayhuash, south of the Cordillera Blanca, Central Peru (19,500 feet).

PREFACE

In recent decades, a trend toward humanistic anthropology has emerged, specifically with the establishment of the Society for Humanistic Anthropology as a section of the American Anthropology Association in 1974. This society and the Society for Visual Anthropology encourage anthropologists to write, film, tape, and use photography during their fieldwork and analysis of multicultural experiences to produce somewhat unconventional ethnographies or written reports and analyses of fieldwork. The Society for Humanistic Anthropology supports a more literary style than previously associated with nonfiction, as well as poetry and narrative forms. The society also encourages the search for authentic narrative voice and methods of expression, such as the notations used by Dennis Tedlock for oral myths and stories, which conveyed that in the performance style of distinctive speech, pauses, and diction, meaning is expressed beyond the words.

While this study is specifically about Andean textiles as visual communication of Quechua beliefs, it necessarily focuses on the contextual use of these textiles in their active roles during rituals and everyday life. In this manner, they communicate meaning beyond cloth. Rituals and textiles may *seem* distinctively different topics for research, but ultimately this is not true. Textiles loaded with symbols are active companions to all rituals. They are not still-life wall hangings, but rather moving, wrapped, layered forms used within ritual sequences, and in these roles they join forces with rituals in the communication of cultural beliefs.

Narrative stories and dialogue seek to unlock meanings in textile and ritual symbols often observed as aesthetically pleasing by the outside world, but incomprehensible when evaluated in the absence of *cultural context*. Through a humanistic approach and an interdisciplinary focus on anthropology, art history, photography, poetry, and creative nonfiction, this book seeks to immerse the reader not only in words but also in the visual reality of Quechuas. While this text presents specific textile and ritual research

Visual anthropology via photography can capture nuances of dress, region, and style such as this Pisaq (near Cuzco) woman in hat adorned with fresh cantu flowers and holding a baby goat.

Maria Merma Gonzalo and her niece Mercedes weaving on traditional backstrap-style looms of the region with Ausangate behind them, village of Pacchanta, Cordillera Vilcanota, Peru (14,500 feet).

from the region of Ausangate, Peru, it more broadly presents examples from other areas of Peru, Bolivia, and Ecuador.

Nonverbal nuances and quick gestures, something captured in an ethnographic photo, lead us back to a truthful cliché that a photo truly is worth a thousand words. The photo provides visual field data as valid as written notes and an indispensable document for future analysis. The Society for Visual Anthropology of the American Anthropology Association is committed to the study of visual aspects of human relations through the use of advanced technology and media as tools for anthropological research, teaching, and presentation.

Photography as an art form and research tool has allowed me to capture not only festival images but also simultaneously the specific use of a particular textile that might have gone unnoticed, making it an invaluable research tool. Generous use of color images in this book has been made possible through the financial contributions of many associates, friends, and supporters for which I am deeply grateful. As a point of clarification, these photos were made over the last twenty-three years. Unfortunately, some individual names are no longer available because the images have been collected in a variety of distant locations, making a return for individual identification difficult if not impossible. Therefore, photographic captions respectfully identify individuals' communities and regional clothing styles. In regard to language and dialect, Cuzco Quechua is referred to unless otherwise noted, as it is the dialect spoken in the region of Ausangate.

The combining of photos, narrative, and personal accounts in a marriage with academic research, data, and analysis is an unconventional approach, but it has enabled me to better convey how art and rituals in some isolated regions such as Ausangate, Peru, reinforce indigenous identity even as the post-modern world tries to fragment them into an urban labor force. For years, I pondered how to express a Quechua view of reality to outsiders who believe that the Quechua world has already disappeared. A strong emphasis on narrative provided a means to let the voices I heard speak for themselves. In addition, images shot right up to the time of publication show cultural forms that still persist in spite of individual, national, and community concerns. In 2001–2002 I returned to Ausangate for several months, where many of the events in the narrative took place, to learn about changes in the lives of Manuela, Maria, Luis, and Mariano, some of the Quechuas with whom I had worked.

Life continually presents humanity with transitions through choices made

A herd of llamas adorned with ear yarns known as t'ikas (flowers) crossing toward grazing areas near Ninaparayoq Lake, northern side of Ausangate (15,000 feet).

by individuals, communities, and societies, but many ancient social, artistic, and ritual forms remain fundamentally intact while paradoxically displaying outward signs of transformation. What works and is retained by a culture creates cultural diversity and in that diversity, identity. As Daniel Quinn (1996) said, "[T]he lifestyle survived because it worked, what didn't work disappeared." Through this study of tactile objects and religious events, efficiency and obsolescence, the modern and the old, I explore what persists and what is adapted along with what is discarded on a daily basis as I attempted to engage the world through the senses as the Quechua do.

The high regard Quechuas living near Ausangate have for the variations, colors, and nature of specific lakes is evident in their conversations and textiles. Ninaparayoq Lake (15,000 feet) near Campa Pass.

Mario Turpo and Luis Pacsi discussing the significance of lake designs on a knitted chullo hat, Ninaparayoq lake region, Ausangate.

Introduction

Luis Pacsi knelt over the textile Mario Turpo held in his hands as the two Quechua men admiringly discussed the fine details of the woven pattern. Luis responded to my question, *"Ari, qochakuna."* I said, "Lakes. Are you saying these patterns are lakes?" Luis raised his arm gesturing toward Ninaparayoq, the large body of water near where we stood at 15,000 feet. He said, "Yes, they are *these* lakes, *right here under Apu Ausangate."*

Being bilingual, Luis continued explaining in Spanish that a *qocha* means more than a *laguna* (Spanish), which I assumed translated to the English word "lake." He related that a qocha is a receptacle for storage of sacred glacial waters melting down from Apu Ausangate, a major mountain spirit and local god. Springs and rainwater are also caught and retained in the qochas. According to Quechua logic inherited from the ancestors, qochas are a type of storehouse for sacred water. Storage of all excess woven textiles, ceramic vessels, and excess agricultural crops, such as seeds, corn, dehydrated potatoes, and meats, was highly regarded during the Inca empire. Spanish chroniclers later mentioned how these large amounts and types of goods were stored and recorded on *quipu*s, a form of knotted and coded cords used for accounting. Luis looked at me, his ethnographer/weaver friend from a world far away, a world of cities and freeways, bottled water and supermarkets, and emphasized what no Quechua person needs to say aloud to another Quechua: "Water is sacred; without it no life exists in the Andes."

Contemporary Quechua people living in the Andes Mountains have inherited a tradition based on beliefs about how individual parts join together to make up a sense of wholeness that is critical to their very existence. While the Inca administrative superstructure no longer exists, some Inca social and communal structures continue to sustain life. But life is more than subsistence. Annual festivals and rituals that attempt to invoke agricultural fertility and rites of passage mark significant stages of life. These events

Weavers, spinners, and knitters work together outside a family's house in Upis (14,000 feet), a village about a half-day's walk from Tinqi, as the children watch and play, north side of Ausangate.

are enriched by the use of costume, finely made clothing, and textiles performing designated roles. Cloth infuses every aspect of life. In daily life, a person may add his or her labor to the land in order to produce crops and tend animals. Cloth is a necessity of everyday health and well-being as protection from the elements since most of life is lived outdoors. Today, labor can still be gifted or traded without involving the use of money in accordance with persistent Inca social structures known as *ayllu* and *ayni*. Textiles are also favored as a reciprocal gift. Reciprocal relationships in which people help one another are critical to life in the high mountains, so for a Quechua person, one of the saddest situations is to live alone. Life is extremely difficult alone in this rugged, harsh, high-altitude environment.

For generations, Quechuas have passed on ancestral information about how to be productive in farming, herding, and weaving. While faced today with choices about what to accept or reject from a globalizing economy, historically they have not been static. Instead they have incorporated changes that they could not resist from outside intrusion or practices that increased their daily efficiency into their traditions in a dynamic manner. "Latin Americans have developed varied and unique cultural forms by constantly absorbing new influences into a bedrock of tradition." (Green 1997:89)

In retrospect, it was in that moment of conversation with Luis Pacsi that I decided I would return to the Ausangate region near Ninaparayoq and to the village of Pacchanta. My purpose was to study weaving designs and techniques to try to understand the ideas and ancestral beliefs that were

Backstrap looms made of wooden sticks and string heddles are used throughout the Andes to weave precisely measured, hand-spun, sheep wool/alpaca, such as this backstrap loom used in Agato, Ecuador.

being encoded into these textile fabrications produced by their hands but informed by their minds and hearts.

In an unconventional twist, I will pause briefly to introduce myself to establish who is relating to and entering into Quechua culture. What are my cultural filters that have informed these experiences, analyses, and writing? The intent is for students, friends, and associates as well as academics to understand how and why we as individuals enter other cultures and report back our findings. Who we are as participant observers informs our results. As John Van Maanen (1988:ix) states about ethnography, "[I]t rests on that peculiar practice of representing the social reality of others through the analysis of one's own experience in the world of these others." While researchers typically are fervent in their discussion of what precisely they seek to explain, Van Maanen raises "more gritty matters concerning why a specific researcher chooses to study a specific social world." (1988:83)

My life revolves around art and woven forms in particular. I was a professional artist successfully exhibiting my work in galleries in New Mexico and California. Inspired by photos in art history texts of Andean textiles from such pre-Columbian Peruvian cultures as Paracas, Chancay, Wari-Tiwanaku, Chimu, and the Incas, when the opportunity to go trekking into the remote Vilcabamba region of Peru occurred, two days later I found myself on an airplane to Lima. I met Quechua weavers, descendants of the Inca people, in their contemporary environments high in the mountains where life was vastly larger than an isolated weaving in a book. Witnessing their daily lives tending herds and harvesting their crops, I sensed that there was a larger context of the weaver's world where these textiles were produced. Thus, I was not surprised when years later I gradually realized that the weavings were a metaphorical presentation of the world they live in. It was a revelation how much information of a mythical or cosmological nature these weavers still encode today in their textiles in this nonwritten way of transmitting cultural information.

Motivated by my first meeting with Quechua weavers, in 1980 I entered graduate school at the University of New Mexico for coursework in pre-Columbian art history and architecture, which helped me understand the Andean quipu, the base-10 mathematical accounting system of knots, and how this might somehow relate to the rules of logic Quechua weavers use today. While expanding my background on the modernization of Latin America from 1850 to the present, I learned methodologies that anthropologists use to study art in other cultures, what oil revenues meant to developing Latin American nations, and the role of the military, among other subjects. I knew that I needed intensive Spanish and Quechua lessons if I ever hoped to understand what they were communicating in these woven records. I pondered how the natural environment of New Mexico had shaped my own work, but then I was not involved in coding ancestral symbols into my weavings.

While still in graduate school, I began working as a cultural guide for Wilderness Travel with a first assignment to coordinate backstrap weaving workshops in Agato, Ecuador, outside the northern market center of Otavalo. Miguel Andrango of Agato had organized a group of men weavers called the Tahuantinsuyo Weaving Cooperative to teach backstrap weaving to foreigners.

Their goal was to revitalize the technical knowledge of backstrap (warp-faced) weaving because European floor looms yielding a different style of weaving (weft-faced) were becoming increasingly popular in the area. Miguel, an enthusiastic innovator in Agato, believed steadfastly in the value of retaining the older traditions. He

Miguel Andrango's efforts to organize a men's weaving group in Agato, Ecuador, for the teaching of warp-faced techniques was an effective means for renewing a sense of pride of identity for weavers in Agato.

Ausangate peak (20,800 feet) from
Palomani Pass. The many faces of this
sacred peak and the surrounding peaks
(locally all recognized jointly as Ausangate)
bond Quechuas in similar livelihoods,
worldview, and lifestyles.

knew the teaching process would renew the men weavers' dignity
associated with the fine weaving of the past. Otavaleños, being expert
business people, are challenged to produce new goods for a rapidly
expanding market for foreign and national tourists. For two summers,
I wove with Miguel and researched the kinds of dynamic changes
taking place in Otavalo due to the significantly increased tourism
attributable to recent improvements in the Pan American Highway
between the capital city of Quito and Otavalo.

Upon receiving my master's degree in Latin American studies in 1984,
my goal was to reside in Latin America as often as I could, especially
in highland communities, to increase my awareness of their particular
way of life. As I gained more experience as a professional guide, I
began leading trekking expeditions into remote areas, such as the
northern Cordillera Blanca around the north face of Alpamayo; the
frigid Carabaya ice cap; the Vilcabamba region near Mount Pumasillo;

the remote Cordillera Huayhaush; and various routes into Machu Picchu including the Mollepata-Salcantay trek and, of course, the famous classic Inca Trail. During this time, my interest in weaving was advanced by the opportunity to collect a vast number of textiles from various regions. My appreciation for the relationship of textiles and their specific uses, including during rituals, grew deeper through interactions with the people. When I decided to pursue my doctorate in Latin American studies, my experiences as a trekking/cultural guide over the many months and years I had spent in Peru were an asset.

While I gained from experiences in all regions, the most important Andean treks for me were those in the Ausangate region, which included climbing over the 16,700-foot Palomani Pass and the 17,500-foot Condor Pass that took me within a stone's throw of Ausangate Peak.

In various situations, including hiking with my husband Ken O'Neil, we gained access to such distant villages as Hatun Q'ero, Hapu, and Kiku. Luis Pacsi and Mario Turpo led us across pathless routes over what seemed like endless hillsides and valleys to the spectacular Lake Sibinacocha at 16,500 feet, which opened doorways into worlds even more remote than I had dreamed. Textile techniques often thought forgotten are still used in those remote places. We saw herds of hundreds of alpacas and llamas grazing in highland pastures; caught fleeting glimpses of wild vicuñas and condors; and beheld Quechua people living in dung-heated, isolated stone and sod houses at over 16,000 feet, who managed to cultivate potatoes as high as 15,500 feet. Whenever I connected a few words of Quechua into a phrase, they smiled broadly and then unleashed long narratives in Quechua at me, such an obvious foreigner. But weaving was the language we spoke best together. At night when I took out my drop spindle, they would come closer to comment on my simple skills, laugh, and then show me their favorite spinning trick and how fine they could spin. The year 2001 marked the twenty-third consecutive year that I have spent three to four months in the Andes doing just what I have described here. I would like to make a parallel with baseball for a moment. One cannot write conclusively on the subject of baseball, for example, just by interviewing and interacting with the players, managers, or umpires.

The actual act of going to the game is an integral and vital part of the whole understanding of the game.

In 1990, I happened to visit Alfonso Ortiz, a Native American anthropology professor at the University of New Mexico (UNM). He told me he appreciated how much time I spent with Quechua people. As a native Tewa speaker, he stressed that conversing in an indigenous language was critical to comprehending the multilevel meanings that certain words possess, and in particular to pay attention to the names of the woven forms and the textile designs. He told me to make every effort to search for those deeper meanings, and then added, "If you really want to understand the textiles, you must study the rituals. You must look for the relationships between the annual agricultural cycles and ritual cycles. They do exist, you know, so look hard for them." That day, with the help of Joanie Swanson and Gil Merkx at the Latin American Institute, I learned that the university had recently introduced a doctoral program in Latin American studies. Within the next week, I was back in graduate school at UNM.

As a mentor over a five-year period, Dr. Ortiz showed me how to more deeply engage indigenous worlds. He reiterated the importance of returning to the Andes often. He asserted that a single field encounter was not sufficient for an anthropologist to profoundly grasp a culture's complex social relationships during rituals and in everyday life. While we viewed Andean slides, he often compared the practices of the Pueblo peoples with the Quechua, especially the Quechua *ukuku* bear character and the clown or trickster in Pueblo dances.

In 1994, with the help of Garland Bills, my first Quechua instructor, I attended Cornell University's summer course in advanced Quechua studies, funded by a FLAS grant. The instructor, Luis Morato Peña, had a well-known talent among linguists for teaching Quechua to non-native speakers. For ten days, he tutored me in the Cuzco dialect before the other students arrived but he maintained his warm direct personal style with the entire class. I could not have had a finer teacher than Luis.

While in Ithaca that summer, I visited with the distinguished Andean

Montera diamond-shaped hat and llicllas
with natural-dyed hand-spun yarns are
worn by an older weaver in the Kilita
Valley (15,000 feet) below Condor Pass,
eastern side of Ausangate.

ethnohistorian John Murra. Sitting outside in his backyard under shade
trees on a Sunday afternoon, he explained that for him, "commitment
to the Andes is what life is all about" and that it requires the deepest
level of commitment. His groundbreaking work in exemplifying the
multiple roles and significance of cloth during the Inca empire is
highly respected, but that afternoon he inspired in me greater determination and hope.

Awarded a Fulbright Foundation grant for dissertation research in 1996,
I became a resident nonimmigrant in Peru and established residency
in Cuzco, dividing my time between reading archival materials and
studying with my Quechua tutor Gloria Tamayo and time in the
highland village of Pacchanta where I studied backstrap weaving with
Maria Merma Gonzalo and her extended family, neighbors, and other
community members. I documented weaving styles on all sides of
Ausangate Peak, traveling from the northern side of Ocongate, which
includes Pacchanta and Lauramarka, to the southern or Pitumarka-
Chilca side. During the grant period, I conducted concentrated field
investigations of textiles and did not work as a guide. My intense
fieldwork periods always remained separate from work as a guide.

By actually weaving with the women and girls, I began to understand
the rich vocabulary of Quechua designs, clothing forms, and techniques.

Flora Clancy, my art history advisor at UNM, had advised me to look
not only at the designs but to investigate the forms of cloth. I often
reflected on Dr. Ortiz's advice to observe how cloth, shaped into
folded and layered forms, moved with the body when I was becoming a godmother or wildly dancing late into the night at weddings
with old women and small girls after I had agreed to
let them dress me in fine local costume appropriate
for these occasions. Surprisingly, I began to understand internally the importance of how costume
affects the wearer in the way it wraps the body, the
precision with how the costume components are
assembled, and how these forms, embellished with
old ancestral designs, move in relation to the human
body. Participation was vital to inclusion rather
than observing from a detached perspective. These
experiences and many others established a foundation of Quechua reality for me that is not written
in textbooks. However, this reality for me was not
a romanticized one in which no one ever gets mad,
shouts during disagreements or fights with their
neighbors, or falls stone-cold drunk into the ditch
for the night. The Quechuas exhibit the full range
of glories and faults of any other human community. They do, however, maintain a worldview of
ancestral teachings with specific rules for dealing
with imbalances of nature and humanity.

In 1997, I finished my Ph.D., and Alfonso Ortiz died
of a heart attack. At the UNM memorial remembrance, his daughter said, "His legacy will live on in
you, his students." Her challenge inspired me to teach a variety of
courses, including Ritual and Symbolic Behavior and Art/Anthropology
at UNM-North and, by fall 2001, I was a visiting professor at Appalachian State University in Boone, North Carolina, where I taught
Introduction to Latin American Studies as well as Art/Anthropology.

Garth Bawden, director of the Maxwell Museum of Anthropology at
UNM, chair of my graduate committee, and an academic collaborator,

Nevado Santa Catalina, Ausangate.
Ausangate is considered an Apu or
mountain god (spirit) to Quechuas from
this area and prayers are offered to the
mountain as far away as Cuzco.

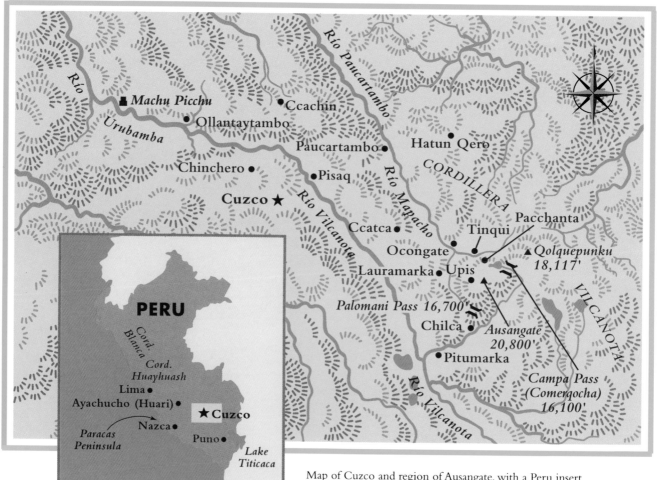

Map of Cuzco and region of Ausangate, with a Peru insert
(Prepared by Deborah Reade)

introduced me to museum exhibits. In 1994, I loaned ethnographic textiles to the museum and wrote text for a Peruvian exhibit that he curated. In 2000, as guest curator of the exhibit "Andean Textiles and Rituals as Cultural Communication," I supplied text and labels, provided photos, and loaned part of my large ethnographic collection of Andean textiles to the exhibit. The exhibit opening in September 2000 coincided with the Textile Society of America (TSA) meetings in Santa Fe, New Mexico. The Maxwell Museum, Latin American Institute at UNM, and TSA combined efforts to bring Nilda Callañaupa from Chinchero, Peru, as a guest indigenous weaver-scholar to speak directly from her heritage at the opening. During that opening, chief curator Mari Lyn Salvador acknowledged the funding award by the National Endowment for the Humanities for the Alfonso Ortiz Institute for Intercultural Studies on the UNM campus.

Remembering Dr. Ortiz's instruction, that "in the Pueblo manner you must tell a story from the beginning," and with this biographical background contextually in place, I now shift directly to the greater part of this book and its primary focus: how Andean beliefs, through time, persist in the telling and retelling of visual symbols embedded in textiles and portrayed in rituals.

The primary regional focus for this book is the area around the important sacred peak, Ausangate, in southern Peru. Ausangate, at 20,800 feet, is the highest peak in the Vilcanota range, approximately eighty-five miles southeast of the former Inca capital of Cuzco.

The peaks around Ausangate each have Quechua names but are often also referred to collectively as Ausangate. The Quechua-speaking people who live close to it as well as the Quechua people throughout the department (province) of Cuzco worship Ausangate as an earth spirit like other Apus, but consider it one of the most powerful. It is often mentioned in prayers and rituals. The people in the Ausangate region are agriculturalists, herders, and weavers bound by a common cosmology and physical proximity to Ausangate. The people ritually feed the mountain to keep their world harmonious and balanced.

The Ausangate region is vast and largely isolated from cities and the modern world. People in the proximity of Ausangate live in stone and sod houses at elevations between 10,000 feet and 16,000 feet. The region's abundant rivers drain to the Amazon basin to the east. The region includes parts of two provinces: Quispicanchis and Canchis. The district of Ocongate in

Quispicanchis has a municipal center in the town of Ocongate. Until thirty years ago, Hacienda Lauramarka was the name used for the entire northern side of Ausangate Peak because the large hacienda officially owned all the land "for as far as one could see" (Luis Pacsi, conversations with author, Ausangate, Peru, 1996), and all textiles from the region were generally identified as Lauramarka regardless of specific village origin. The area is accessible by truck or occasional bus from Cuzco over the dirt road to Puerto Maldonado, and the trip by vehicle takes about six to ten hours to Ocongate depending on road conditions. All local or regional official documents or licenses are obtained in Ocongate. Rural inhabitants walk hours out of the mountainous areas to the center for Sunday market or legal documents. Goods are shipped via truck for Sunday markets in Ocongate and Tinki. The town of Pitumarka in the province of Canchis is the principal municipal center for Quechuas living on the southern side of Ausangate. Access to the southeast side of the mountain requires a half-day trip in a sturdy vehicle over a rough dirt road, and then walking on footpaths for days is necessary to reach Chilca (Chillca) or Lake Sibinacocha. No major marketplaces exist in the highest-elevation areas of Ausangate, and no roads penetrate the region.

Traders, traveling with the traditional llamas and now horses, have been bringing powdered chemical dyes into the highlands for fifty to one hundred years, but natural dyes are still used in places like Chilca. Due to the region's extreme geographic isolation, the textile symbols, forms of clothing, and technical processes remain strongly linked to the people's environment and their ancestors.

The weavers produce certain textile forms and designs not found elsewhere in the Andes, and their textiles remain a tie to the ancients. Very little, if any, written documentation of Ausangate textiles exists to date. Ann Rowe (1977a) studied Pitumarka textiles, but did not have the opportunity to go up into the Ausangate highland area. Gail Silverman-Proust investigated the Q'ero symbols (1988; 1999) but did not continue with an investigation of the Ausangate region. Katharine E. Seibold (1992) worked with women weavers in Choquecancha near Ccachin outside of Cuzco, but this area has distinctively different symbols from Ausangate. While the scattered inhabitants surrounding Ausangate Peak are the major focus of this book, textiles and rituals from other areas near Cuzco are discussed when appropriate.

Before continuing with an in-depth discussion of contemporary weaving, understanding the duration and durability of the fine heritage of Andean textiles is vital. Weavers are part of a connected series of civilizations and ancestors. This period of time is replete with cultural, political, and historical upheavals specific to the Chavin, Wari, Tiwanaku, Chimu, and Inca civilizations, followed by the Spanish conquest, colonialism, independence, modernization, and now globalization trends. Through all of this, weavers have continued to create textiles. Andean pre-historical heritage and modern history are woven like the threads of a fine tapestry into a story whose parts are joined by the shared continuous inhabitance of a mountainous environment by indigenous peoples.

The Quechua language is at the heart and forms the glue of highland life in Peru, as do the large herds of camelid animals in their symbiotic relationship with man and land. Camelid fibers and coastal cotton were woven into textiles for many centuries before the Spanish brought sheep that were adopted by Quechua herders. Old technologies of drop spindles, backstrap looms, and other weaving devices were supplemented by the European floor loom but not forgotten. The use of clothing to establish identity is a persistent communication of Quechua ethnicity. Modern tourism and consumer markets mandate cultural contact with others, but trade has always been an essential part of existence. While tradition disguises itself under a mask of dynamic change, it does not disappear and it does not die as quickly as some imagine. It is capable of transformation within *its own forms.*

After an examination of Andean heritage, the land and animals, weaving techniques, specific meanings in symbols and forms, social structures, pilgrimage, festivals, and rites of passage as related to textiles, this book concludes with the influences of the modern, post-modern, and global economy on the indigenous Quechua. They maintain their own set of rules or logic, their engrained habits deeply embedded inside that fabric of cultural values. "The whole is greater than the parts" applies to Quechua reality. Thus, this book concludes with a final serious consideration of why this Andean tapestry has survived centuries of change and conquest, through everything from Latin American militarism to a tidal wave of post-modernism. My hope is that this book will help develop the perspective and knowledge of people with a wide range of interests in Andean culture, those who are just being introduced to it, and experienced Andeanists.

Three varieties of women's shoulder cloths or *llicllas* from Pacchanta, north side of Ausangate, each measuring approximately 20" x 22". These llicllas are smaller than those of other regions near Cuzco and show some of the diversity of the diamond motif. (Photos by Pat Pollard)

TEXTILES

Man's poncho from Hatun Q'ero near Ausangate with textual close-up of lake motif displaying sun symbols inside each lake. (Photos by Pat Pollard)

CHAPTER ONE

Textiles as Visual Metaphor and the Anthropology of Art

Weavings through both their structure and symbols are visual metaphors representing the meaningful relationships that Quechuas form with nature, animals, and the environment so that Andean life as a whole can survive. Individuals work together to produce a unity of purpose much as weavers join together yarns to create strong textiles to warm bodies, wrap babies, carry goods, and make sacred ritual offerings. All family members participate by spinning the long oily alpaca and sheep fibers cut from the animals' bodies into strong double-plied yarn. Pairs of women laboriously count and stretch the yarn, investing hours in preparing the warp structure before they actually start weaving. Precise color placement is required to enable the weaver to be able to later pick up certain colored yarns to form the patterns. She applies her acquired knowledge of culturally appropriate symbols and her technical skill to express her ancestral concepts of how the world as they know it survives through periods of chaos and order.

The concept of worldview as elaborated by Redfield (1956:85–86) is "a group of conceptions . . . the way a people characteristically look outward upon the universe. The culture of a people is, then, its total equipment of ideas and institutions and conventionalized activities. . . . Worldview suggests how everything looks to a people, the designation of the existent as a whole." José María Arguedas (in Stephan 1957) said, "The Inca's worldview included a sense of order, grace in design and integration with natural forces and shapes. The Andean world view takes its roots in the past, but lives, survives and persists in the present."

Worldview is persistently expressed through the medium of cloth in

some Andean villages. In the context of movement during rituals, festivals, or daily activities, symbols understood by the community are displayed and have meaning to the learned. Communication through symbols and recognized shapes of cloth conveys an understanding about cultural ideas or an expressed worldview.

New symbols and shapes are introduced today in this time of globalization and manufactured clothing; however, indigenous identity and Andean textile tradition are habitually reinforced by the continued creation and sustained use of handmade Andean cloth. Quechua weavers practice skills learned from their mothers, grandmothers, and great-grandmothers, and many can still identify the mythical meanings of each distinct symbol. In some regions, a specialized vocabulary exists for the type, shape, and meanings of particular symbols. Weaving in these ways is the vessel through which many teachings are transported and publicly displayed. Persistent nonverbal expression of ancestral beliefs through art forms such as weaving is quite remarkable in today's rapidly homogenizing world, in which expression is more typically written.

Pacchanta lliclla and close-up detail of bright colors preferred by some weavers with white beads (pini), ric-rac (qenqo), and sequins added to adorn textiles. The shiny materials are said to reflect the sunlight when worn just as light shimmers on lake surfaces. (Photos by Pat Pollard)

Being a weaver myself, I anticipated that the introduction of synthetic yarns and chemical dyes might signal the diminishing value of textile arts, but Maria and the other weavers quickly taught me that their choice of available imported materials did not necessarily indicate a loss of Quechua aesthetics. Maria said, "We use synthetics because we like the bright colors." Their material choices were evaluated according to their own aesthetics, the aesthetics of the Ausangate region, which place high value on lasting, vibrant colors. As with many indigenous people worldwide, the efficiency of techniques and the usefulness of materials and objects can be crucial not only to survival in severe environmental conditions but also to local aesthetics. Aniline or synthetic dyes are called *polvos,* Spanish for dust, and they are more easily transported, easier to make, and are more fade-resistant than natural dyes. But ease of use is not their only appeal, and the same weavers who use the synthetic dyes often painstakingly re-spin commercially bought yarn until the spin is fine enough for local aesthetics. One spinner told me, "The synthetic yarn is ugly. We re-spin all of it." I asked, "[T]hen why do you buy it?" He replied, "I like the colors and it is the *moda* [style]." Another

Ccatca, a village en route to Ausangate, is unique in the continued production of ikat ponchos as shown in this close-up detail. Ikat is a rare process in Peru where the designs are not created by a pick-up technique, as are most Quechua warp-faced textiles, but depend entirely on the pre-weaving dye processes. (Photos by Pat Pollard)

said, "[W]e like sequins because of the color and they reflect the light; it shimmers like the surface of the lake."

Where the materials come from is not as important as the role they play or their utility. Natural fibers are highly valued because they are of the animals and their fibers are silky and long, but not to the exclusion of an imported color or fiber that adds pizzazz to local aesthetics.

I soon discovered, while weaving and living with Maria, her sister, Valentina, and other Pacchanta weavers, that my own worldview was a detriment to a deeper understanding of the Quechua worldview. I decided that it would be better to set aside some of my own ingrained aesthetics to more fully comprehend *their* vision of the world through local aesthetics. Quechua culture does not have a use for the word "art," at least according to the twentieth-century Western definition; textiles are rather aesthetic forms used to express a worldview that is not divorced from the function and utility of the object. In his introduction to *Anthropology of Aesthetics* (1971), Jacques Maquet said that anthropology would be enriched "by an inquiry into aesthetics and a better understanding of art." Maquet traced the large collections of material objects that were accumulated, documented by monographs, and placed in museums in the late 1800s. He wrote, "None of these items was considered to belong to art. . . . The unabridged gap between savage and civilized is taken for granted, and obviously art was on the civilized side." (1971:3) Referred to as primitive art in the early twentieth century, indigenous objects became art by designation when outside collectors, museums, critics, curators, art dealers, and Western audiences acquired it, thereby removing it from the original cultural role in the society that created it.

In the 1950s, anthropologists and ethnologists began to focus more attention on how to deal with the academic study of art and artists in contemporary cultures throughout the world with greater concern for the social relations of artists in communities, processes of production, and the expressed aesthetics of the artisans and users of the art objects. The idea of studying material culture as social process gained strength. (D'Azevedo 1958) The obvious advantage of ethnographic studies of contemporary cultures is that researchers can observe or participate in the processes of production within the cultural context and question the craftspeople and artists directly about their aesthetics, choices, and meanings of symbols. Artisans may not answer questions with direct responses, but through participation and observation in their lives and crafts, the potential exists to learn their categories and the basis for the choices they make. The artisan's reluctance

Maria Merma Gonzalo teaching the author how to weave complicated warp pick-up designs or *pallay* in her courtyard, Pacchanta.

to answer questions may indicate more about the nature or form of the questioning than the artisan's unwillingness to answer.

Clifford Geertz (1976:1487) stated that art objects are a way to materialize experience, that "the visual patterning and habits of society are a result of the relationships that exist." Changes observed in symbols or shapes over time, materials selected, and even techniques and interpreted meanings may indicate communal choices or an individual's decisions based on nonconformity to cultural norms, simply individual expression, or adaptations to outside influences. "All innovation involves a dialectic between convention and invention." (Babcock 1982:226) Once, when I tried to weave plain weave instead of design to fill in the last two inches of my design to terminate a bag, Maria informed me, "That is not correct, take it out." It was the only time that we significantly disagreed. She would not allow me to vary from the local standards for a finely executed textile. Just as a mother is judged by the behavior of her children, as my teacher, she would be judged by the correctness of my detail. The criteria of basic skill and understanding of "rightness" are judgments made by peers within the community of textile production.

Material expressions embedded in cloth are communicative forms used by women weavers in indigenous cultures. They surface in Western culture from time to time. Judy Chicago, a North American artist/feminist, likewise states that "art is communication," but she pressures Western art critics and audiences to include needlepoint as art when she uses a "thread as a brush stroke." She advocates expanding the boundaries of art or craft, departing from the definition of art as exclusively the mediums of sculpture and painting. She states that weaving has the status as a less expressive form within Western art traditions. (Chicago, 2001) For Westerners, material expressions of culture through textiles have cultural boundaries to overcome to become recognized as art, but Quechuas easily acknowledge the value of visual representation of their worldview in woven textiles through an inherited understanding of expressive culture.

Woven messages can include information about social oppression and resistance or nonconformity to social norms. A form of stitched cloth in Peru known as *arpilleras* includes visual images of police beating up protestors and strikes against the educational system, along with social statements such as nude beaches, overcrowded buses, soccer matches with Coca-Cola advertising, and simply herders tending large flocks.

Cloth can be the drawing board, the visual shout of injustice. Cloth should not be overly romanticized as only having sweet statements of "the world as it is." The continued production of Inca styles and designs into the eighteenth century, until colonial legislation outlawed it after the uprising

Arpilleras are cotton-backed, stitched remnants of fabric used to create fabric collages and, like woven textiles, are capable of communicating visual messages about Andean culture. This message of social resistance and protest depicts a strike scene in front of the Ministry of Education with the police hitting people, a woman fainted, police vehicles, and protest signs. (Photo by Jon Hedlund)

of Túpac Amaru II, testifies to its role as a form of resistance. Textiles, like all art, not only express the view of the world of the artist or group but also, at times, "resistance or covert expressions in coded messages within their art forms." (Radner 1993:vii) Similar to the rules for operating a computer or the interpretation of certain words, in some instances rules must be followed to obtain the desired result. When people wish to express values related to a worldview, the rules must be precisely observed. Without adherence to the rules, communication is misdirected. Why does the artist, weaver, or locksmith create? What is the intent? Is the intent correctly received by the audience or do they interpret based on their own experiences?

The concept of a closed society is evaporating with globalization, but a society intent on bringing forth survival skills and religious beliefs that worked for the ancestors may choose to quietly continue practices unobservable by the rapid-paced "other" world. How can observers not connected to the indigenous world spend a short period of time with them and achieve a deep understanding, even if they are academics? Researchers lack the tools for understanding indigenous cultures when armed only with ethnocentric Western attitudes. My concern here is textile arts, however, as forms of communication that, covertly or openly, have the potential to speak in many voices through the coded information placed in them by their makers and to be understood by the users and local audience. The critical factors are the continued practice of making the cloth, coding the designs and forms, and memory of their meanings.

Contemporary Andean Textile Research

In the last twenty years, researchers have produced a small body of work about indigenous textiles in the Andes. The broader concept of costume as communication gained fresh attention when Margot Blum Schevill published *Costume as Communication* (1986), an exhibit catalog for the Haffenreffer Museum of Anthropology, stressing that clothing, body adornment, textiles, and cloth are powerful indicators of social structure, ritual patterns, economic networks, and a commitment to traditional life. Schevill, Berlo, and Dwyer later edited an anthology of articles, *Textile Traditions of Mesoamerica and the Andes* (1991), which opened academic discussion of the communicative aspects of cloth and costumes.

In the early twentieth century, the field of anthropology had neglected the study of material culture other than to form large collections for museums. Anthropologist Ronald Schwarz (1979:23) stated that, "Clothing is a

Weaver from the Pitumarka valley revitalization program works while her son watches and learns about textiles from his mother.

subject about which anthropologists should have much to say, yet remain mysteriously silent." He called for "anthropologists to develop a foundation and methodological approach for the anthropological study of clothing and adornment."

As of this writing, more than thirty years later, Schwarz's argument for an "anthropology of adornment" has yet to materialize. Weiner and Schneider (1991) investigated the contextual roles of cloth in communication, identity, gender, folklore, power, tourist production, wealth, virtue, symbolism, and politics in large- and small-scale societies worldwide. Many exhibit catalogs and textile articles have been published in the last thirty years, and another volume would be required to discuss them all. Some exhibit catalog essays have made important contributions, such as *Andean Aesthetics* (1987) by Femenias (Elvehjem Museum); *Weaving for the Gods* (1999) by Brinckerhoff (Bruce Museum); *To Weave for the Sun* (1992a) by Stone-Miller (Museum of fine Arts, Boston); *The Extraordinary in the Ordinary* (1998) by Kahlenberg; and *Traditional Textiles of the Andes* (1997), edited by Meisch (DeYoung Museum).

While specific exhibit catalogs contribute valuable essays illustrated with some color images, large art historical texts are funded to include many color plates of pre-Columbian textiles with essays on structural analysis. The second volume of essays and color plates in the two-volume set, *Andean Art at Dumbarton Oaks* (Boone 1996), is devoted entirely to textiles in the collections, many donated by Robert Bliss. Yoshitaro Amano produced an impressive publication, *Textiles of the Andes* (1979), with text and color plates of

This Chilca man's poncho, made from naturally dyed yarns in the Upper Pitumarka Valley, is typical of the all-natural style textiles for which Chilca is famous. Symbols include lakes, corn, plants, and flowers. (Photos by Pat Pollard)

the large collection displayed by the Amano Museum in Lima. Integra AFP, Wiese Bank, and Aetna funded the definitive, 844-page *Tejidos Milenarios del Peru* (Lavalle and Lavalle 1999), which includes numerous color plates of pre-Columbian textiles, as well as colonial weavings and some contemporary ethnographic textiles in the article by Gail Silverman (1999).

Ethnographic research provides a link of past to present by providing contextual in-depth studies of weaving in specific communities today. Among the most notable are Lynn Meisch, Ecuador and Tarabuco, Bolivia (Meisch 1987; Rowe 1998); Elayne Zorn, Bolivia and Taquile, Peru (1987); and Katherine Seibold, Choquecancha (1992). The Textile Museum in Washington, D.C., has published the proceedings of the Irene Emery Roundtable on Museum Textiles, including *Ethnographic Textiles of the Western Hemisphere* (Emery and Fiske 1977) and the *Junius B. Bird Conference on Andean Textiles* (Rowe 1986).

One article, however, is a milestone for Andean textile research: "The Semiology of Andean Textiles: The Talegas of Isluga" by Veronica Cereceda (1986). She notes that while questions have been asked about "techniques, use, chronology, style, and spatial and ethnic distribution[,] . . . the specific language of the fabrics has been ignored." (1986:149) She also expresses a unique perspective: "Can a traditional Andean textile be viewed as a text, not only as decoration . . . but [also] as a specific message behind which lies a system that explains the message? What are the conventions of this code?

What are its minimal units? To what extent is the woven text comprehensible within but also beyond the Andean communities in which it has been elaborated? Cereceda says, "[I]n a sense clothing carries a double function or role: communication carried in the fabric and sometimes a magical religious rite that can affect the objects held inside the fabric, in the case of clothing, the human body and soul." (1986:149)

As I came to understand in Pacchanta, another role of cloth is transmitted by the active use of the piece. In other words, the object cannot be separated from the idea or metaphor that it communicates for the people who understand the system of communication being used; otherwise, it becomes only a decorative object. Cereceda's research focused on the organization of woven space and the significance of formal elements and supplied future researchers with an approach on which method could be constructed. In more recent years, she co-founded the Foundation for Anthropological Investigation and Ethnodevelopment (ASUR) in Sucre, Bolivia. The present work of ASUR is carried out with indigenous weavers of the Jalq'a and Tarabuco communities to produce and market high-quality forms of traditional textiles. The sale of these textiles through the ASUR museum shop provides income for weavers from both regions. Her contributions to textile research go beyond academic parameters in an illustration of how researchers can give back to the communities they study.

Mari Lyn Salvador's (1978) methods for studying *molas* of the Kuna (Cuna) women in the San Blas Islands of Panama suggest a research method through visual anthropology. Salvador assembled a variety of samples of textiles from the region. She then asked a group of women to rank them from best to worst and describe the reasons behind their rankings in order to stimulate uncensored discussion and generate an open expression of local aesthetics.

How indigenous peoples are stimulated to create what they make is a prime focus of this text. A study conducted over a long time period reveals outward signs of change but makers themselves must be asked why the changes occur. What is or are the basic unit or units of expression? In oral traditions, children learn sound units rather than letters. The basic unit is not obvious, and decoding the small variations within units reveals information on the language and culture. How do weavers construct statements with the knowledge of these units? Is a symbol merely a condor, puma, llama, or lake, or is it more of a mnemonic device like the *quipu* for the memory of a myth, narrative, or teaching story? Asking the right, often simple questions presents one of the greatest challenges to researchers.

Why do weavers make what they make? Some indigenous people persisted in making and wearing ancestral styles of clothing even under the threat of severe punishment. The colonial era in Peru is an example. What influences are local markets and manufactured clothing seen on television having on the expression of Quechuas' unique identity through clothing and textiles today? How does attendance at local rural schools affect the use of traditional or ancestral clothing?

During the course of my research, I saw that some young people were forced to migrate to the cities in search of jobs because of terrorism, remnants of the old hacienda land system, and increasing population pressure on family land. Clearly, it was difficult to maintain their weaving skills and textile heritage if they were forced to accept wage work as maids and household help. At the same time, some communities were busy organizing weaving revitalization programs to help maintain respect and dignity for the Andean textile heritage that dates back thousands of years. This heritage is the core of Quechua integrity.

Contemporary woman's carrying cloth known as a *kaypina*, displaying intricate pick-up design work from Calca, Sacred Valley near Cuzco. (Photos by Pat Pollard)

CHAPTER TWO

Andean Textile Heritage

Without a doubt, the art and
manufacture of textiles constitutes
one of the most significant achievements
of the ancient peoples of Peru.

—Lumbreras (1974:17)

Contemporary Andean people possess an exceptionally long heritage of communicating their worldview through rituals and textiles. Beliefs concerning the agricultural, social, and religious foundations of Andean life have been woven into textiles, knotted into cords, painted on ceramics, and incised in gourds for millennia. Pre-historic Andean people constructed fiber baskets, sandals, gauze, ropes, and bridges for functional everyday use, but they also embellished cloth with meaningful geometric symbols, abstract designs, and composite figures representing the mythological ideas of their makers. Readable text using a written alphabet was not found when Europeans encountered the Americas.

Why was writing not developed? From a research point of view, we are asking the wrong question. Comparatively speaking, consider the breakthroughs made by Mayan epigraphers in the last twenty years in the comprehension of Mayan codices and glyphs as historical records. This indicates a more significant question concerning the use of forms, perhaps linked more to mathematics and visual symbolism, instead of writing to record events, persons, and epic or cataclysmic change. Could they have used tactile

Ccachin woman's carrying cloth woven from natural hand-spun wools, Lares region near Cuzco. Typically, Ccachin textiles are red- and orange-dyed fibers, making this a rare specimen. (Photos by Pat Pollard)

surfaces rather than paper to record symbols other than alphabetic letters? Could they have found something more efficient in their unique environment than letters for the recording and transport of information? Could there have been information coded in weaving that we still cannot understand? Would a computer discovered as an artifact 2,000 years from now reveal any more about its former contents than the textiles do now?

Artifacts intrigue archaeologists and art historians with ancient symbols painted on wooden drinking cups and boards, molded into ceramics, etched into gourds, and woven into fabrics that indicate some system of communication that no longer communicates to its contemporary audiences. The keys to the codes are lost except in the odd fascination of indigenous artists who continue to use techniques related to ancestral traditions. We cannot assume that a diamond pattern from a weaver 2,000 or more years ago means the same as a diamond pattern in Ausangate today. But we can say that symbolic representation has been going on for several thousand years with apparent communication of meaningful information in symbols recorded in cloth. Whether cloth is "text" or not captivates us today, but it is an unimportant question for Quechua weavers. They know that cloth communicates cultural metaphors, myths, and beliefs. It is their heritage.

Peru happens to be one of the world's richest storehouses of ancient textiles. The frigid Pacific Humboldt Current (also known as Peruvian Current) off the Peruvian coastline has created an exceptionally dry coastal desert almost devoid of annual rainfall, providing a climate perfect for textile preservation. Peru's oldest known textile fragments dating from around 8600 B.C. were found in the dry Guitarrero Cave in the central Cordillera Blanca mountain chain. (Lynch 1980) The northern coastal site of Huaca Prieta in the Chicama Valley has disclosed textiles dating between 3100 B.C. and 1300 B.C. with design motifs almost identical in form to those used well into the Inca period. While the symbolic nature of these motifs is undeniable, their exact meaning is unknown today. In 1946, North American archaeologist and textile specialist, Junius B. Bird, discovered more than nine thousand textile and cordage fragments at the northern coastal site of Huaca Prieta. His codification and analysis of this extensive data were a major contribution to the study of Andean archaeological textiles.

It is important to remember that archaeological dates for Peruvian textiles rely heavily on radiocarbon methods and the use of a relative chronology developed by John H. Rowe (1967a). While carbon dating is one approach to the study of material culture, relative chronology allows for a comparative placement of materials into categories of stages or units of cultural similarity. Relationships of objects to each other are based on stylistic changes presumed to be chronological or to demonstrate a linear progression in terms of refinement. Whether simplified line, form, and design indicate early development is still controversial among art historians and will undoubtedly continue to be a topic for discussion.

Art historians generally refer to time divisions called horizons, defined as periods of expansive artistic, military, or political influence. For the Andean region (occasionally designated as the Pan-Andean), the three great horizons are defined as Chavin/Early Horizon (1400–400 B.C.), Wari-Tiwanaku/ Middle Horizon (500–900 A.D.), and Inca/Late Horizon (1200–1535 A.D.). Horizons encompass a vast expanse of ideas and symbols over a large geographical area. Periods of contraction, in contrast, are associated with more regional art and craft production and influence. North coast Moche and Chimu and south coast Nazca and Paracas exemplify contraction. Throughout the contractions and expansions of empires in pre-historical eras, a high level of sophistication was achieved in artistic endeavor, which had sacred, functional, and artistic roles and forms. As far as we know today, art was not separate from the functional.

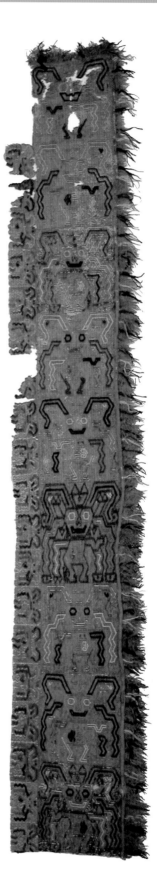

Peruvian art history is an immense endeavor. In this text, archaeology and textile heritage are discussed to firmly establish the links among fabric, knots, yarn, and woven forms as communicators of cultural information. Andean archaeology continues to catch the world's attention with exciting discoveries, such as the Lord of Sipan burial site in the north coastal Lambayeque Valley, excavated by Peruvian archaeologists Walter Alva and Susana Meneses. This recently unearthed Moche site has revealed spectacular ritual costume details adorned with gold and gold artifacts. High-altitude archaeological discoveries by Johan Reinhard from 1995 to the present made public the Inca frozen sacrificial mummies that the world later came to know as Sarita and Juanita. Having been frozen for centuries on glacier tops, the mummies' perfectly preserved woven garments challenge textile scholars such as William Conklin of the Textile Museum in Washington, D.C., to develop techniques for carefully unveiling the frozen textiles so richly coded in symbolism. In the northeast high jungle in Chachapoyas, intact mummy bundles wrapped in cloth survived climatic changes; today, *huaqueros,* or grave robbers, and archaeologists compete to see who can get there first to retrieve precious textiles and artifacts. Peruvian archaeology remains in process with new finds being made almost daily. When these new finds are made, the relative-chronology dating system has given researchers a degree of flexibility necessary to catalog and place new finds within an existing array of found artifacts.

Art historians have had a long fascination with Andean art and symbols, including major contributions by Wendell C. Bennett in the 1930s, Alfred L. Kroeber in the 1940s, Junius B. Bird in the 1950s, and Elizabeth P. Benson and George Kubler in the 1960s. From the 1960s until the present, John H. Rowe of the University of California at Berkeley and John V. Murra of Cornell University have trained many graduate students in Andean studies while they formulated their own concepts about Inca woven symbols known as *tocapu,* and uses of cloth during the Inca empire period. William J. Conklin has contributed significantly to the understanding of visual representation

Fragment of a Paracas textile (0–100 A.D.), cotton with camelid fibers. Collection of the Maxwell Museum of Anthropology, University of New Mexico.

in Andean textiles through the concept of "structure as a carrier of meaning." He suggests that researchers' preconception that there must have been a written language with some resemblance, such as an alphabet, to our own may have created an obstacle to understanding the "other modes that involve formal visual constructions that were used across the culture and conveyed complex meanings." (Boone 1996:321)

> Visual imagery in the Western tradition is characteristically thought of as secondary to written communication, as illustration of the basic story that is always told in words. The Western world considers this relationship between "word" and "image" as the very definition of "normal." . . . But there is evidence to suggest that in the Andean world not only the design but also the structure of textiles directly conveyed ideas. [Conklin 1996:321]

Ann P. Rowe, curator of the Western Hemisphere Collection at the Textile Museum in Washington, D.C., has meticulously categorized the types of structures in ancient Andean textiles (1977b) as well as such contemporary collaborative investigations as *Costume and Identity in Highland Ecuador* (1998). While this book deals primarily with contemporary weavers and textiles, it acknowledges the valuable contributions of the too-numerous-to-mention studies of art historians and textile specialists who have contributed substantially to the field of Andean textile expertise. Among these, Anne Paul (1990), in her study of Paracas textiles, supports the concept of woven forms or fabric art as vehicles for communication of worldview.

> The "texts" of Paracas culture are its embroidered garments, for the rows of repetitive images on those weavings are ideograms that functioned somewhere between writing and pictures of things. [Paul 1990:78]

Paracas textiles date from approximately 500 B.C. to 500 A.D. South of Lima between the Pisco and Ica Valleys along the Pacific coastline, Paracas is a dry, windy peninsula with a unique climate caused by an unusual occurrence of the cold Peruvian Current hitting the warm land outcrop. Nearly devoid of vegetation, it has a daily weather pattern of foggy mornings, windy afternoons, and cold nights. The cold Humboldt Current from the south supplies abundant fish and sustains fish meal production today as a subsistence activity. Nearby Nazca reveals not only extraordinary geometric lines and figures created by ancient peoples, but the remnants of an extensive underground channel system for irrigation and cultivation of crops. (Paul 1990)

While the entire Peruvian desert coastline has extensive burial sites and tombs, during the 1920s Peruvian archaeologists Julio César Tello and Toribio Mejia Xesspe found undisturbed, intact Paracas mummy bundles. These bundles have led researchers to verify that Paracas weavers depicted metaphorical animals and anthropomorphic characters through a large repertoire of symbols, and that animals, plants, and composite beings seem to have been used to convey a sense both of identity and of worldview. (Paul 1990; Peters 1991) During the 1980s, Anne Paul received permission to systematically unwrap still-intact bundles warehoused at the Museo Nacional de Antropología, Arqueología e Historia in Lima by Tello and Mejia in 1927–1928. She discovered a deliberate order or placement of objects in relation to the other items in the bundle. (Paul 1990:9) The contents of these bundles are the main record of Paracas culture since its members left no written record. Covered with rows of isolated images, the garments worn by the rulers or placed in burials were a fundamental form of visual communication within Paracas society. Paul suggests that the Paracans believed that the ancestral spirits residing in the earth continued to contribute to the welfare of their communities. In Paracas, as in other Peruvian cultures, these complex ideas were transmitted in the cloth of woven garments. (1990:16) Paul concludes that "dress is a form of communication, functioning as an overt expression of identity: anyone who is literate in the styles of weaving, in the codes of dress, and in the designs woven into cloth in these communities is able to read instantaneously about the wearer. Embedded in terms of apparel are visible indicators of such things as ethnic group, ayllu affiliation, cosmology, economic status, gender, age, family ties, marital status, and offices held within the community." (1990:17)

Creation of visual symbols to express cultural identity or ethnicity and the sharing of common origins, beliefs, language, or group definition of belonging has old roots in Peru. The fabrics are the clues left by deceased artisans. The artisans are gone but the textiles remain. Consider for a moment the cross-cultural expression of identity through woven textiles in the world today even with the availability of mass-produced fabrics. Humanity shares a commonality of expression of ethnicity and identity through clothing choices.

The advanced textile techniques developed by artisans such as sprang, embroidery, and feather work indicate a highly sophisticated knowledge of textile expertise (Bennett and Bird 1949:127–28; Bird 1954) continuing into the Middle Horizon. A symbolic system of repetitious units with slight intentional pattern variations displaying contractions and expansions appeared to represent elaborate metaphors in Wari-Tiwanaku textiles. (Sawyer 1963) Were important individuals, the feats of heroes, or epochs in Andean civilizations represented in images in some manner of disguised symbolism? Could the contractions, expansions, and juxtaposition of symbols possibly have been visual metaphors for historical or political events representing the natural contraction and expansion cycles of history, administrations, or empires during Wari-Tiwanaku?

> At first these bold comparisons seem to celebrate geometry itself; their designs read as grid-based, rectilinear, strikingly coloristic, dynamic and above all, *illegible* pattern. . . . However, by delving deeply into the artistic system it is possible to recognize many of the actual images as well as geometric forms that make up the expressive system of the Wari (Huari), a state that controlled most of Peru during this time (Middle Horizon). . . . It is the artistic process of abstraction— one of the most intriguing in all creative endeavor—that unites readable imagery and relentless pattern in to a complex aesthetic. [Stone-Miller 1992a:35]

Abstract symbols have stimulated researchers like Alan Sawyer (1961; 1963) and John Rowe (1979) to look for standardization of abstract textile motifs by systematically analyzing regularities of design elements in specific prehistorical textiles from Nazca and Inca periods. Ann Rowe's (1977b) manual of weaving structures details techniques from the S-warp ikat to supplementary and discontinuous warps, warp substitution, derived float weaves, complementary and compounded warp weaves, double weaves, and composite structures, and is an invaluable reference. Technique can be understood, while abstraction in designs, as deliberate as it was, remains largely undeciphered.

Inca Textile Antecedents

Historical documentation of Andean textiles began with the Spanish chronicles, written accounts by priests, secretaries, and other Spaniards of their perceptions of the New World. "Andean art did not correspond in any sense to European notions of representation." (Cummins 1994:190) The aesthetics of the two worlds clashed in many ways. Abstract representation communicating information to the Inca in tactile knots, painted boards, wooden cups, weavings, and painted ceramics was not always understood by the chroniclers, but their documents have allowed researchers such as ethnohistorian John Murra to elaborate for the benefit of art historians and archaeologists the multipurpose roles and performances of cloth in the Inca world. "Cloth was so important in Inca culture that it was characteristic of Inca insistence in and of itself. At every turning point in the life history of the individual cloth played a key role." (Ascher and Ascher 1981:66)

Murra (1962) recovered information about the social, political, and economic significance of cloth during the Inca empire by examining the large body of historical documents left by the Spaniards. The primary concerns of the Spanish-Catholic influx were gold, greed, and personal wealth, but conversion of the Andean peoples to European religion, values, and their vision of history was also a major objective. These handwritten documents provide a record of Inca practices even if they do not contain the Inca version.

Institutionalized reciprocity of cloth and state distribution of cloth as gifts were fundamental in the Inca empire, and the state needed the people's labor, in the form of tax tribute through cultivation of land, to produce sufficient food and a steady, reliable supply of textiles. The state distributed land usage rights, weaving materials, and food to the populace. State storehouses functioned like banks where the Inca ruler controlled the deposit and withdrawal of goods. Cloth was the preferred gift of gratitude and played an important role in rituals. The Inca ruler could display institutionalized reciprocity and gratitude for special merit by generous gifting of fine textiles. The value the Inca military placed on garments was so great that taking enemies' clothes symbolized defeat and death. (Murra 1962) Chroniclers Garcilaso de la Vega, Pedro de Cieza de León, and Padre Bernabé Cobos, among others, attested to the high value placed on cloth by both the state and individuals. "A great number of people worked to provide the weaving specialists with the necessary materials; the entire society seems to have been involved in the task." (Gayton 1973:282)

Inca society's exceptional sense of administrative organization and order enabled the empire to expand and govern the diverse peoples absorbed into the state. Murra developed a theory about the importance of the exchange of goods among the various ecological zones ruled by the Inca. He found that the needs of individual ethnic groups to complement their own ecological resources could be met and enhanced by controlling and exchanging

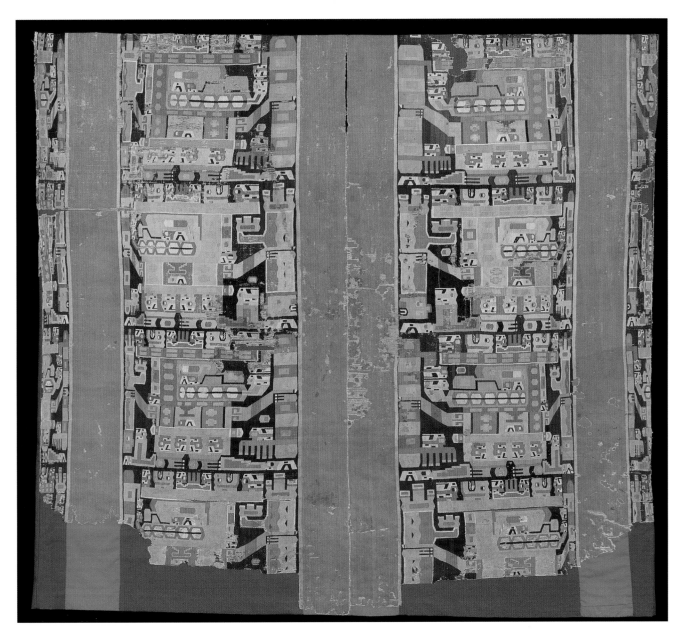

Huari (Wari) tapestry shirt or man's tunic from the South Coast dating 650–800 A.D., camelid and cotton fibers. Dumbarton Oaks, Pre-Columbian collection, Washington, D.C. Photograph by Justin Kerr.

Inca men's tunic-style clothing with woven *tocapu* patterns and design elements as depicted by the sixteenth-century chronicler Guamán Poma.

resources with people from other ecological zones. Trade relations existed among people living at sea level, at 16,000 feet, and at elevations in between. Thus, highlanders could enrich the quality of their lives by exchanging their salt, meat, animal products, grains, and potatoes and other tubers for coastal seafood, and tropical jungle foods such as fruit, coffee, corn, and peppers. Llama convoys traveled immense distances transporting goods across lands of competing ethnic groups ruled by the Inca empire. Each ethnic group was incorporated into the state as a separate Inca administrative unit with local government left to regional lords. Newly acquired citizens were given gifts of highly prized cloth to wear, thus initiating relationships of reciprocity and obligation and establishing the Inca principles of duality and reciprocal exchange. (Murra 1980a)

State warehouses where food, textiles, seeds, and numerous other goods were collected were an institutionalized solution to food supply problems and the need to sustain the population in times of famine, drought, poor harvests, and other natural disasters. Many of the high-altitude agricultural regions have only one growing cycle and only one marginal, annual crop. In these areas, storage means survival. The methods used to freeze- or sun-dry surplus Inca crops to last through the year are the same that Quechuas use today to preserve their crops.

Quipus, knotted records that tallied the stored treasury, were sent to Cuzco by runners with exact accounts of warehouse inventories. Fine cloth and

Inca man's tunic with checkerboard pattern (1476–1534 A.D., camelid fibers). Private collection

other goods were sent to Cuzco as well, in quantities more than necessary to supply the elite permanent residents of Cuzco. (Murra 1962:717–22) Craig Morris believes one reason the runners went to Cuzco bearing surplus gifts was so that the surplus would be sent back. The value of the returned surplus goods was greatly increased by association with the Inca nobility and with the imperial city. (Morris 1986:64)

Commercial markets and monetary exchange were likely nonexistent in the central and southern Andes during Inca rule. According to Morris (1986:49), the distinction is between exchange of goods and tribute versus trade as commerce. No formal marketplaces were found because goods were exchanged in a system of informal barter. (Morris 1986:61) Today the informal market sector in Peruvian cities thrives outside of formal affiliations. The exchange of goods from the various ecological zones often occurred in August after harvest. Reciprocal relations of the Andean village were basically enlarged upon to govern the economic system of the Inca empire. (Morris 1986)

Growing populations and increased territory challenged the Inca state. The state cared for its military on the move with clothes, tents, blankets, lances, darts, sandals, and gifts from the warehouses for service. Textiles held extraordinary prestige even for military service, which included the guarantee of two garments in return for fighting. (Montesinos 1644, cited in Murra 1962) Feather cloaks were highly prized for military excellence and stripping off of clothing was a harsh punishment for prisoners or captives.

The state needed military control but also a social, political, and religious mechanism for balancing the opposing forces of the physical and supernatural world. Male shamans acting on the Inca's behalf and the Inca himself used ritual to enter the supernatural realm and mobilize the spiritual force of the ancestors or the natural world on the people's behalf. Specialized cloth was essential to these rituals.

Women made cloth for their families and for ceremonies, and were sometimes cloistered for these and other duties. Local lords reinforced Inca alliances by marrying women of the Inka lineage, thereby making them principal wives. (Morris 1986:51) The House of the Chosen Women or *acllawasi* consisted of a special class of cloistered women weavers who wove and prepared food for the administrative centers as well as the Inka himself. Daughters of allies would be accepted into this chaste existence and consecrated their lives to the gods. Regional capitals that had temples dedicated to the Sun also had an *acllawasi* nearby, where as many as two hundred virgins lived with their *mamaconas*, literally "esteemed mothers." After a careful selection process, the most noble and beautiful girls were given specialized education until they reached the age for service to the Inka. The mamaconas taught them state duties, Inca religion with its rites and ceremonies, as well as women's duties, such as technical knowledge to spin the finest yarn and weave sacred textiles used for clothing to dress idols, cloth for sacrifices, and special garments to be worn by the Inka. (Cobo 1990:172) This specialized hierarchy of weaving skills and knowledge was privileged information.

Inca weaving was based on ancestral heritage but included its own symbols through repetitious and systemized geometric units composed with a fine sense of order and precise detail. According to Mary Frame (1986), the careful choice of repetitious geometric units and their arrangement, including the use of negative space, by Inca weavers was imbued with specific meaning. She believes that meaning through placement of icons or symbols has been consistently employed in textiles since the Inca empire period to the present. She argues that Inca bands taken as a whole give examples of how the grids and symmetries of fabric structures operate as a construct for the conceptualization of space, giving it form, diversion, direction, and unity. This manner of filling both field and border had meaning and represented a whole system composed of related but distinguishable parts. (Frame 1986:55) Asymmetries, color, count direction, yarn twist, and symmetry all have meaning in code-like form and are calculated to communicate a worldview, including concepts of time and space. "The structuring processes used to order chaotic, loose fiber into utensils and shelter may have provided a tangible model for understanding and reflecting observed structures and phenomena in the natural world." (Frame 1991)

Organization and order of individual units, whether in textiles, people's labor, or food, were the cornerstones of Inca philosophy. Morris (1986:64) said that the importance of Inca organization as a philosophical approach to state administration was evidenced by how the Inca recorded people and goods for political and economic accounting and administration of public projects such as large-scale buildings and road construction. Two Inca textile forms, the tocapu and quipu, demonstrate Inca logic and order.

> Within the quipu, we can show by the groupings of these categories what the priorities were in the thinking of Andean peoples: first come the people, second the camelids, then the cloth, fourth the ceramics and so on. For a people who have made a natural refrigerator, survive at freezing temperatures, build bridges as a community

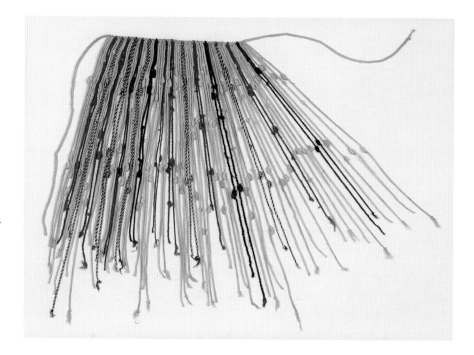

A mathematical base-10 knotted system for recording numbers in the hundreds of thousands recorded by Spanish chroniclers to have been used as a memory device for the telling of Inca oral history. Collection of the Maxwell Museum of Anthropology, University of New Mexico.

task and still weave and maintain a status system based on the fineness of cloth, to investigate this world, we must follow Andean thought and language patterns. You have a logic, not our categories nor a historical one but Andean logic. [Murra 1980b]

Inca accounting and the telling of epic Inca narratives were aided by the quipu, a tactile arrangement of knots and cords using a mathematical base-10 system. (Ascher and Ascher 1981) In the 1920s, while studying a number of quipus from various museums, Leland Locke discovered a consistent code related to the kind of knot used that helped him realize that certain knots represented numbers in the hundreds of thousands. (Locke 1923) A highly trained group of specialists, the *quipucamayocs,* were responsible for creating color-coded cords with carefully constructed, strategically placed knots for decoding information and retelling oral narratives using quipus as mnemonic devices. (Cummins 1994:194) The detailed analysis of quipus illustrates how Inca specialists used a tactile device to enhance oral tradition and numerical codification.

Today, Quechuas continue to rely more on visual stimuli than accounting ledgers or textbooks for education or memory enhancement. Vendors in the Saturday market in Otavalo, Ecuador, for example, knot codes into the straps of the hundreds of netted *shigra* bags they sell to help them remember the price they paid. Value embedded in a system of knots is reminiscent of

About eighty years after the Spanish conquest, Felipe Guamán Poma de Ayala wrote a 1,179-page letter to the King of Spain, in which he inserted 397 drawings including these drawings. As a native Andean who grew up under Spanish rule, Guamán Poma de Ayala's purpose was to inform the King of Spain about the abuses and corruption introduced by the Spanish. His visual text of the Inca state has been invaluable to Andeanists. Left: Chief treasurer and accountant. Right: Secretary to the Inca and the Inca's council.

Source: Marcia Ascher and Robert Ascher, *Code of the Quipu: A Study in Media, Mathematics, and Culture* (Ann Arbor: University of Michigan Press, 1981), 45.

the logic of the quipu. (Cobo 1990; Ascher and Ascher 1981) Only informed members of the society can or could distinguish the communication code in both the quipu and in textiles, past and present.

Tocapu refers to abstract geometric designs with standardized square or rectangular units found in certain finely woven Inca textiles used in men's tunics (*unku*), women's dresses (*anaku*), and cloaks worn at important Inca ceremonial occasions. Variations of tocapu existed, including several rows of pattern on a solid background; an upside-down, stepped pattern on top; totally patterned garments; other times tunics were simple black and white checkerboard squares or the distinctive Inca key motif. Tocapu can be as simple as a repetitious motif of alternating colors and as complex as the one illustrated here. A sense of order is implicit. Cummins (1994:198) states that tocapu probably demarcated ethnic, political, and religious status, but the Spanish chroniclers did not see the abstract images as recording Inca histories because the abstractness of the tocapus did not correspond to the Spanish chroniclers' perceived ideas of how an image *should look*. Unable to understand the design information, they did not record its details. Sarmiento and Molina (in Cummins 1994:199) suggest that certain painted boards recorded tocapu design elements and were used by Inca judges. The persistence of tocapu in portraits of Incan nobles for two hundred years after the Spanish invasion attests to its cultural importance as the predominant "script" of the

Inca man's tunic with all-t'oqapu (tocapu) design dating from 1140–1540 A.D., camelid fiber and cotton.
Dumbarton Oaks, Pre-Columbian Collection, Washington, D.C.

empire. (Rowe 1967b:265) Possibly the Inca nobility did not share explanations of tocapu designs with the Spanish invaders. Tocapu was defined as a royally granted privilege and as such was highly prized by rulers and the military alike. (Murra 1962:720)

Eighty years after the arrival of the Spaniards, Felipe Guamán Poma de Ayala wrote a 1,179-page letter to the King of Spain, which included 397 drawings. Apart from actual tocapu weavings, his drawings are the best visual record of the woven designs. He recorded that the tocapu consisted of rows of rectangular or square geometric designs in a pattern of repetition. The juxtaposition of many of the units in the Inca tocapu demonstrates concepts of repetition, inversion, and reversal, while the use of black and white and color expresses duality and balanced opposition, and, the use of red accents to denote the Inka, the color generally associated with him. John Rowe (1979) detected regular, precise, apparent standardization in the patterns given to intentional irregularities and an asymmetrical balance in colors, numbers, and forms in the arrangement of the tocapu. Textile specialists continue their quest for a Rosetta stone leading to the decoding of Inca information in woven tocapu according to the rules of Inca logic, but few cloth examples of tocapu survive today. MacArthur Fellow and anthropologist Gary Urton is currently using a mathematical approach to investigate Andean logic and quipus, but we do not yet understand the tocapu code. Tocapu was also painted on the wooden drinking cups called *keros*, and researchers at the Universidad Nacional de San Antonio de Abad in Cuzco continue to work with the tocapu in their museum's collection of over 200 keros.

Over time, Andean record keeping has taken many diverse forms, from burning and etching images on gourds of courtship, marriage, medicinal practices, weaving and the arts, herding and cultivation, death and other rites of passage to painting Moche designs showing virtually every aspect of daily and ritual life onto ceramics. (Donnan 1978) Material objects surviving from the past, including some of the world's finest textiles, give us glimpses of Andean peoples' beliefs and their worldview regarding the natural physical world, and their symbiotic ties to animals and the spirits.

North face of the pyramid peak of Alpamayo
(19,300 feet), Cordillera Blanca, central Peru.

Herd of alpacas gathered in
a stone corral, Lauramarka
Valley near Ausangate.

CHAPTER THREE

Geography, Animals, and Agricultural Cycles

Peru is a land of vast geographic diversity, ranging from the long, dry, and narrow Pacific coast desert with its irrigated pockets of green cultivated vegetation to the 22,000-foot snow-capped peaks forming the extensive Andean *cordilleras* or mountain ranges.

Deep shadowed valleys cut the mountainous chains and glacier-fed lakes punctuate the *puna* or high-altitude grasslands. The eastern Andes drop dramatically off into the *ceja de la selva,* the high jungle, and finally disappear into the cloud-covered humid Amazon basin. Survival in such diverse climates and geography requires efficiency and cleverness. In the highlands, for instance, the expression *chiri wayra* (cold wind) is muttered aloud as cold winds whip up the valleys almost daily. Certainly *chiri* (cold) occurs every night at elevations of 14,000 to 16,000 feet where frost, hail, and snow are frequent and warm protective clothing is essential for existence.

The Peruvian Andes are an extreme, vertical environment made barely habitable by subsistence farming and extensive herding of large numbers of South American camelids, the alpacas and llamas. Traditionally, alpacas have been domesticated for their fine soft hair while llama hair is coarser, used primarily for ropes, saddle blankets, and heavy woven sleeping blankets. Quechuas cut the animal's hair in summer at the beginning of the rainy season before the heavy rains, but the hair is spun into yarn throughout the year. A third type of Andean camelid is the skittish nondomesticated vicuña. Vicuñas are highly prized in Peru as well as internationally for their hair, a fiber similar to cashmere in softness, which is used to make elegant coats, ponchos, shawls, scarves, and cloaks. Poachers greatly reduced the wild herds,

Llama train transporting cargo of
potatoes in Upper Pitumarka Valley.

Smoke from cooking fires seeps through the thatched roofs of sod houses in Uchuy finaya,
with large herds of alpacas and llamas nearby.

but the Peruvian government established large reserves; at present vicuñas are no longer an endangered species. The fourth type of Andean camelid, the guanaco, is relatively sparse in Peru.

The animals subsist on the native plants, such as ichu grass, which grows at the higher elevations where cultivation is limited. Over time people have formed a symbiotic relationship with the animals in order to co-inhabit this land.

Quechua speakers who refer to themselves as *runakuna* (the people, humankind) use the animals' hair for warmth and clothing, the pelts for beds, the dung for heat and cooking fuel, and the meat to make *charki* (sun-dried jerky). For these reasons, the animals are absolutely essential for human survival in this radically vertical geography. It is an isolated, difficult world, yet a stunningly beautiful natural environment.

Indigenous people live in the highlands at 9,000 to 16,000 feet in scattered clusters of adobe, sod, and stone houses. At the lower end of the altitude range, they grow corn, squash, beans, peas, and other vegetables, but in the higher elevations only potatoes and other tubers can be cultivated. Potatoes can be cultivated up to about 15,500 feet, but these are not the sweetest or most highly prized varieties for which Peru is famous.

The Andes are geologically young mountains, often with sharp, craggy peaks and high passes called *abras* or *nudos* (knots). Life is dominated by a vertical orientation. Human beings ascend and descend mountain trails on foot constantly. Because roads have

The animal dung used for cooking and heating fuel is stored in cone-shaped structures to keep it dry during the rainy season.

been built through some valleys, Quechuas occasionally cross mountain passes in the backs of heavily loaded Volvo or Mercedes trucks atop produce and freshly cut wood from the jungle or cases of Cuzqueña (local trade name) beer from the city, but walking is the most common form of travel. Europeans introduced horses, which are still used to transport cargo. Foodstuffs such as surplus corn, potatoes, or other crops are carried on horseback to market, and manufactured goods, such as plastic wash bowls, synthetic yarn, kerosene, sugar, flour, rice, and other goods are transported home.

Prior to contact with the Spanish, llamas were the traditional Andean beasts of burden for transporting goods across the Andes. Llama trains are still spotted transporting goods to and from markets such as Urcos, one hour south of Cuzco. Alpacas have never been used to carry cargo but instead continue to be domesticated primarily for their soft hair and pelts. Their meat is rarely eaten except during special festivals. On the other hand, even though llama meat is made into charki, the Quechua diet is not rich in meat.

From the moment an animal's throat is slit as its life is sacrificed for food, every part of the body is conserved, including all of the blood. During

certain festivals and rites of passage, an animal may be slaughtered to cook in a *pachamanka*, an outdoor earthen oven made from stones. The pachamanka is used only once, since it is completely destroyed in extracting the meat. The cut-up seasoned meat of an entire sheep or other animal is placed inside with potatoes or *oca* and sealed tightly during cooking. On a daily basis, protein-rich grains, such as *quinoa* and *kiwicha*, are eaten in soups rather than large portions of meat. The animals are more valu-

Earthen oven known as a pachamanka, constructed entirely of stones in the fields, is used to cook an entire sheep and potatoes on special occasions.

able alive as a source of hair and sign of wealth than eaten for meat, so killing of animals is done sparingly and with discretion.

Historically, the Incas used llamas in long animal trains to transport potatoes, salt, hides, and meat to the jungle and coast in great trade networks. Extensive trade among the diverse geographical zones enriched the lifestyle and balanced the nutrition of people within each zone. For example, in the Ausangate region, huge llama caravans passed through near Lake Sibinacocha on their way from Puno on Lake Titicaca to Markapata in the lower jungle. Throughout the Andes, highlanders were able to trade for coffee, bananas, manioc (*yuca*), cacao, coca leaves, mangos, oranges, papayas, and other tropical foodstuffs from the lowland jungle. In the ceja de la selva, the eyebrow of the jungle (4,000 to 7,000 feet), where the climate is still semi-tropical, bamboo, ferns, orchids, and a wide range of native plants and many unclassified wild flowers thrive.

Between 7,000 to 10,000 feet, a different range of cultivated crops are possible via a cooperative effort of the Pachamama (Mother Earth) and the seeds planted and nurtured by Quechua farmers. These crops include favas (broad beans), maize (large-kernel corn), squash, lettuce, cabbage, peas, beets, as well as wheat, barley, quinoa, and other nutritious grains. While neither markets nor money existed in the Inca empire, exchange still occurred via barter or trade relations similar to those still used today in Hatun Q'ero near Paucartambo to the north of Ausangate. In August each year, foodstuffs such as peppers, corn, and squash cultivated by Q'ero families living in the jungle are transported to Hatun Q'ero at 10,000 feet. Hatun Q'ero is understood as the "center" ground for these people. Relatives of the same families or other Q'ero families return with high-puna goods such as meat, potatoes, and animals. Spanish chroniclers recorded the practice of great trade gatherings that occurred in August after the harvest and freeze drying of potatoes.

Multi-colored Andean corn known as *choclo* is boiled for food or fermented to make local corn beer called chicha. The dried husks and field stalks are used as animal fodder.

According to John Murra, control of various ecological zones was probably a central motivation for political and economic unification in Inca and pre-Inca states. He developed a theory called "vertical archipelago," which describes a strategy for food distribution within a single vertical communal system. People living in the same community but at different geographical levels maintained family relations and social ties with food producers in other zones. Based upon these relationships, they exchanged various products of their specific zones. (Murra 1972:427–68) Barter and trade of foodstuffs rather than monetary exchange continue to be an integral part of agricultural practices as described in the Q'ero region. In addition, some people also go to Sunday market in Ocongate and others travel to Cuzco to sell their old textiles to tourists.

The Relationships of Agricultural Time and Ritual in the Andes

The division of labor is in agricultural time for the men and in pastoral time for the women. For men, the passage of time, the difference between any two days is marked by the cycling and duration of

Andean crops are often cultivated on extremely vertical terrain. The dramatic variation of the annual wet and dry agricultural cycles is visible in these lush green fields of the rainy season (ABOVE) contrasted with the dry plowed fields (FACING PAGE) of Pitumarka ready for planting as the rains approach.

different agricultural duties and the growth of the crops; for the women time is marked by the alteration of pasture lands and the growth of the animals. Thus the annual pattern of grazing can be characterized as a rhythmic expansion and contraction centering on the community. Because the seasons are also closely related to the sequence of agricultural duties, such as planting and harvesting, the pastoral cycle is integrated with the agricultural cycle. [Urton 1988:19]

For most Andean areas above 10,000 feet, a twelve-month period yields only one agricultural cycle. The climate varies from sunshine to hail the size of golf balls to drowning rain, all of which affect crop yields. Andean people speak of only two real seasons: wet summer and dry winter. Planting is done in late September to November for most crops just before the beginning of the rainy season in November.

The warm wet season from November to March/April is the growing

Harvesting potatoes in Chilca, Upper
Pitumarka Valley.

Chilca man, making chuño, stomps the
moisture from the potatoes at midday
causing them to shrink daily as they freeze
again each night. Within several weeks,
enough water has dehydrated so that the
chuño can be stored for at least a year.

season. While timing varies for different crops, the valley land is generally
ploughed for corn in September to November with planting in December.
Fava beans are planted in October/November but barley, quinoa, and wheat
are ploughed and planted in December/January. Tubers are ploughed in
September/October and then planted in October/November. All plants
require care and weeding during the rainy season. May and June are the
harvest months for the majority of crops except for early-yield varieties.

In July, potatoes and other tubers are made into freeze-dried *chuño* or
moraya, depending on the type of tuber. They freeze at night in the open
courtyard and as they heat up at midday, people stomp the moisture out.
Through this repeated daily process, the potatoes are made ready for storage
for up to one year and llama meat is made into charki.

In the dry season, the animals must be moved to higher ground for
sufficient forage. Women and children shepherd the animals during high
grazing. August is also the month to re-thatch worn roofs. During the dry season,
animal dung must be collected, dried, and stored in small, sod, conical-
shaped huts for fuel during the rainy season. Animals are brought home to
stone corrals near the houses for both their safety and to make dung collection
easier. Finally, in September, tools are repaired, field preparations completed,
and some planting begins as the cycle repeats itself.

Planting songs are important at this time as are agricultural predictions
made by ritual specialists based on the weather in the first twelve days of
August. Quechuas respectfully call the land the Pachamama, literally, the
Mother Earth, the living mother of all life. The ways in which humankind
treats the mother corresponds to her reciprocal yield of crops. Prediction
and proper offerings at the right time ensure that plants will grow and nour-
ish animals and people. The Pachamama is considered a female Andean deity representing the feminine principle in origin mythology, with power
over agriculture and a companion for women in weaving, spinning, and
cooking. (Núñez del Prado 1974:246)

After the harvest every June, the earth is dry when no rains come.
Pachamama is hungry and must be fed. In a rite known as *cabañuelas,* the local
ritualists (*misayoqs*) make offerings to the Pachamama with their predictions
for the new agricultural year. They offer *pagos,* literally payments, in the form
of strong prayers accompanying material gifts of food, port wine, and *trago*
(sugarcane alcohol), and other items considered vital to planting procedures.
(Núñez del Prado 1974:250) The first of August predicts the month of
January; that is, if the day is rainy and wet, then January's weather will be the

same. The second of August then foretells the weather of February, and so on for ten more days. Some ritualists continue in repeated cycles of twelve for the entire month of August but everyone knows that the first twelve-day period is the critical one for predictions and offering gifts in the hopeful anticipation of the Pachamama's reciprocity of fertility and good crops.

The agricultural and ritual cycles are intimately interwoven and cannot be separated. Over a long period of time, Quechuas have formed certain patterns of relating to nature, paying their respects, and asking for favors such as fertility from the mountain gods. Superficially, Catholicism is the dominant religion, but ancient animistic rituals are still practiced in the Andes despite fervent attempts by the Spanish to obliterate them. Animism is the belief of the spiritual life force or energy in all natural forms, including trees and other plants, rocks, boulders, raging rivers, mountain glaciers, stagnant pools, lakes, and high peaks.

What Westerners call inanimate or lifeless forms are alive to Quechuas who demonstrate a profound respect for the spirits of mountains and the earth in their rituals and prayers. Quechua people are in awe of earthquakes, thunder and lightning announcing the rains, mountain streams speaking in voices, and thundering avalanches. Unusual natural phenomena, such as boulders that seem to have wind-carved faces or twinned ears of corn, are seen as signs from the gods.

Quechua people believe that life depends on balanced relationships with nature for good crops and abundant herds. For them, all life comes from the Pachamama and in death returns to her. She shelters the ancestors, that is, the dead and their spirits. In a wide-ranging definition of Pachamama as space-time, she seems to encompass the past, present, and future.

Rivers carry water from the peaks, springs, and lakes downward to the sea. Pitumarka Valley, Peru.

In the Andean worldview, agriculture is not possible without offerings by ritualists with specific duties, and weaving, herding, and community cannot be separated from the whole of ritual. As Alfonso Ortiz had told me, you must look for the old ritualists and you must try to understand the interrelatedness of all aspects of life. You cannot study weaving as something separate from the rest of Quechua life. All beginnings and endings require a blessing or assistance in realigning energy.

Mariano Turpo Condori reading coca leaves while making a despacho to send to Apu Ausangate, outside his home at Alkaqocha near Campa Pass.

The highest class of Andean ritual specialists is known as an *altomisayoq,* and through ancestral training they are believed to possess the ability to speak directly to the mountain spirits and natural forces on behalf of the people. Quechuas believe that when crops are ruined from hail, floods, or drought, someone or something has caused an imbalance with the natural world of the spirits. If a state of imbalance exists, it is necessary to seek the assistance of a *misayoq,* and preferably an altomisayoq, to correctly make a *despacho* (literally, dispatch), that is, an offering or pago on behalf of the people.

The despacho is offered late at night by burning it and letting the smoke carry the prayers to the mountain gods. All misayoqs have powerful associations with the Apus, but individuals usually associate with a particular Apu. They perform specific duties corresponding to the level of training they have achieved. Misayoqs have survived many trials, such as being hit by lightning, severe illness, or near death. The *pampamisayoqs* focus on healing illnesses through knowledge of herbal cures. Some misayoqs, such as Mariano Turpo, divine the future by reading coca leaves.

Before I participated in a despacho and the blessing of my work in Ausangate, I had done some valuable research on different types of textiles from various regions over the years. But when I experienced the sending of this pago to Ausangate on my behalf by Mariano Turpo, along with his advice on how to live in Pacchanta, opportunities opened up for me. Alfonso Ortiz's advice about the necessity of studying rituals to understand textiles became real for me. After this event, I no longer only hiked through the region, I stayed.

A Personal Story of Ritual

In 1996, I met Mariano Turpo Condori, the highly respected altomisayoq in the Ausangate region who lives near Campa Pass (16,100 feet). I had hiked over this pass many times in the previous ten years. Perhaps I had even seen the eighty-six-year-old Mariano vigorously chasing his grazing herds in the high pastures near the pass, but I did not realize that he was an altomisayoq respected by people in places as far away as Q'ero and Cuzco.

While in Cuzco preparing to leave for Pacchanta, I ran into Juan Víctor Núñez del Prado while standing in line at the Banco de la Nación. He is an anthropologist from the Universidad Nacional de San Antonio de Abad and the son of the famous Cuzco anthropologist Oscar Núñez del Prado who studied the Q'ero people in the 1950s. When I told him I was leaving soon for Ausangate, he told me to ask Mariano how I should approach studying weavings in Pacchanta. Juan said, "Ask Mariano to send a pago for you to Apu Ausangate praying for permission to live there and that your time will be productive." He told me that Mariano lives near a lake called Alkaqocha.

I pondered where to begin this search but was rewarded when my old *arriero* (pack animal owner) friend who knows this region well, Luis Pacsi, remembered Mariano from his childhood. He said that about forty years ago his father had gone to retrieve Mariano Turpo to come to their village of Mahuayani to make some pagos because their crops were poor and the animals were dying. He told me that he thought Mariano was more or less eighty-six years old, but that some people living in Pacchanta (three hours walking distance down the valley from where he lives) think he is over a hundred years old while others comment he looks much younger. Ages are always hard to determine in the Andes and many people do not know how old they are.

Mariano lives alone in a one-room stone hut with a thatched roof near Alkaqocha (black and white lake), the highest of the upper lakes above Pacchanta, where he herds his many animals in full view of

Nasario Turpo, Mariano's son, preparing a pago or despacho to bless the land and for Apu Ausangate.

Ausangate. From his hut, it seems that he could reach out and touch the 20,800-foot Ausangate peak. I have heard some skeptics around Cuzco speculate that no altomisayoqs exist anymore, believing the highest level to be pampamisayoqs. However, in the Ausangate region, people know that Mariano communes with the gods on their behalf, and assert that he is really the only one who can give you an audience with a mountain deity.

Luis took me to see Mariano who consulted the coca leaves (*watoq*) and agreed to do the pago I requested. Coca is a legendary bush grown on the eastern slopes of the mountains and is a well-known, highly prized trade item among Quechuas. Coca plays a social role when mutually exchanged as people sit and chew it communally. Coca cannot be separated from ritual or the Quechua worldview. Coca is a sacred plant, the plant that alleviates thirst and hunger. It is a gift the gods shared with the people. When read by a misayoq, coca leaves foretell the solutions to one's problems and future events. The use of coca dates back to Inca rituals and is still used constantly in contemporary rituals.

After consulting the leaves, he told me that my work and time living here would be favorable. Coca leaves were placed in an *unkuna* cloth, a rectangular, finely woven piece of natural alpaca with no design other than stripes and pampa, or broad open spaces. He folded the cloth ends inside to form a smaller closed square something like an envelope. As his hands moved, pulling the folded flaps open, some coca leaves stuck, others were inverted and some had fallen into new positions. He carefully studied the patterns and positions of particular leaves and their relationships to one another and then interpreted their meanings. He inquired if I had questions and I asked who the best weavers in the area were. He replied, "Maria," and told me to go live with her. Luckily, I already knew who he was talking about from years ago when she had shown me various textiles near the Pacchanta hot springs. He consulted the coca leaves one more time and told me that I was preoccupied about something but not to worry because it would work out fine. He was absolutely right; I was extremely concerned about the new Fulbright grant and how I would proceed to learn more about the textiles.

He instructed me to face Apu Ausangate Peak where he would send the pago on my behalf. He said, "This pago is to feed the mountain." He started by saying Quechua prayers with an occasional Spanish word interspersed while chewing coca and searching through the small folded despacho packets that we had purchased from the curandera in Cuzco's central market, to see what was in each one. Luis assisted him while my husband Ken and I watched. He precisely cut the large unbleached piece of paper that came with the packets into smaller square pieces, in exactly the sizes he wanted. Next, he selected various objects, such as seeds, threads, pods, small crosses and rice, carefully placing them in precise relationships on top of the paper. It was similar to an artist making a painting or a collage where each aspect must be in relationship to the other parts for the meaning to be correct. "The fat of the llama chest bone is a delicacy," he said, "something special to send." He picked small rectangles of shiny gold and silver papers, small cookies, crosses, coca, and huayruro seeds from the jungle.

Suddenly he said, "Did you bring flowers?" We had forgotten fresh flowers. He looked disappointed, dug into his woven shoulder bag, and then got up from the blanket where he sat outside the stone corral and went inside his house. After some time, he finally returned holding some dried flowers (at 15,500 feet, flowers are not easy to find). He said, "These will do." He selected a few grains of white rice and some quinoa, then added bits and pieces of other foods. "It is important to feed Ausangate what the Apu likes to eat," he said. He added, "I know what Ausangate likes to eat in the same way Andrea knows what Ken likes to eat."

Opening a bottle of port that we had been instructed to bring, he put some in the cap, saluted the Apus, gave more to the offering, and drank a little himself. He added *trago* (cane alcohol) followed by a few drops of the red wine. He continually stuffed more coca into his mouth taken from his alpaca-skin coca bag (*pukucho*), the kind only misayoqs can carry, while he continued praying and gestured with his waving hand. He blew over the leaves in the direction of Ausangate. Occasionally, he drank a little more port and offered it to us. We, of course, drank and mimicked what he had done toward Ausangate.

Finally, when he was pleased with the combination of objects and prayers said, he sprinkled a bit of sugar over the top of everything, and folded the paper closed. Mariano took a delicate gold string from the packet, and then tied it around the despacho and put the offering respectfully inside a protective *unkunita* textile (a small, finely woven piece specifically for pagos). He hid the cloth with the offering under the corner of the weaving where he sat. Hidden deep inside it was an assemblage of minerals, soil, pods, beans, seeds, sweets, rice, noodles, small images, fat, clay, shiny letters, cookies, candies, and the flowers, which we were grateful he had found.

During the several hours of ritual he made three different despacho bundles. Clearly, the quantities of each thing he selected were as important as the placement. Often he placed only a seed or two, or several little cookies. He did not use all of each little packet. Number was important in the selection of everything, even the carefully selected *k'intus* of coca with six leaves in four groupings. He joked and laughed aloud with Luis and us while he made the pagos, but retained a sense of the sacred and a serious nature throughout the ritual. After he folded the third paper in on itself securely, he suddenly said, "We are finished." He told us that later the same night he would take the pago to a particular place higher in the mountains where he would burn them. He said the smoke would carry our requests accompanied by prayers to Ausangate. He mentioned several times during the process of making the pago that this was not a game. A badly made despacho can do harm. He said firmly, "Some people think it is a game but it is not."

Luis, Ken, and I descended down the mountain trail to Pacchanta, where I asked Maria if I could study weaving and stay with her. She agreed right away. Later that month, I returned to Pacchanta alone but with the blessings of the pago sent to Ausangate by Mariano. Mariano continued to be an important force in my life in Pacchanta, even though I did not see him often. Life was fairly smooth. He and Ausangate gave me a good beginning.

CHAPTER FOUR

Social Structures, Language, and Daily Life

Pacchanta, a three-hour climb 2,000 feet uphill from Tinqi, the small, local Sunday market center on the road to Puerto Maldonado, became home. After some time, distinctive patterns of interactions and social obligations were revealed to me. Houses in Quechua villages are grouped together in one place. They are clusters of stone, adobe, or sod thatched-roof houses spread over distances with various families joined together by social obligations called ayllu. The Incas used this *ayllu* system of organization to delineate individual claims for land and water rights based on labor relationships inherited from past generations. One's labor is still valued today for its reciprocal exchange with other members of the ayllu. The ayllu communal organization extends far back in the archaeological record. (Moseley 1992:51) It has survived the economic and political changes of the Incas, Spaniards, Republicans, and Reformists. (Bastien 1978) Ayllu membership continues to define certain rights and relationships basic to communal survival and extends these relationships beyond blood ties of an extended family. At birth, a person inherits a set of relationships to others and claims to labor, land, water, and other resources. (Moseley 1992)

While scholars may not agree on an exact definition for the ayllu, it remains important to Andean people as a functioning order for their social relations and obligations. "By living on the mountain and ritually feeding its shrines, people become a part of the mountain ayllu, village or country.... [T]he ayllu is extended beyond the kinship ties of the region." (Bastien 1978)

Experiencing the ayllu brings one closer to its real meaning. In my role as godmother to thirteen children in Peru, I now belong to several Andean ayllus through relationships of *compadrazgo*. Being part of an ayllu is a serious Quechua responsibility. The children's families told me that I am part of

Becoming a madrina and *comadre* during a first haircutting rite in Pacchanta.

their ayllu as a "spiritual co-mother for the children who is concerned with their well-being." The obligations of *madrina* or Quechua godmother include baptism, first haircutting, sixteenth birthday, weddings, and such things as school clothes, fixing teeth, paying doctor bills, and being a family domestic counselor for the parents as well. The responsibility for the well-being of the child is shared not only with the parents but also with aunts, uncles, cousins, grandparents, and all other blood relatives. They say, "You were not born here but we share spirit now." These reciprocal obligations work in both directions. As a godmother, you are constantly overfed at social events and expected to get outrageously drunk with your compadres on *chicha* corn beer, trago, and Cuzqueña beer. It is impolite to reject food and drink because they are making a gift of their very best for you. Rejection would be interpreted as a statement that what they are offering is not a good enough gift for you. A godmother must become clever in how to say no in a gracious manner.

Ritual is essential to the ayllu. Ritual maintains integration among society, earth and religion; it is a process that enables these peoples to express through symbols their oneness with the mountain. They feed it and eat it. They become the mountain and the mountain becomes them. Wearing symbols of the mountain, they dress like the mountain that gives them their clothes and the designs for the clothes. Their oneness with the mountain is their integrity. [Bastien 1978:xxv]

Thatching a new grass roof for one of
Maria's houses, Pacchanta.

Labor promises are understood through a surviving Inca social structure
called *ayni* where no money is paid and no written contracts exist, but
rather nonverbal understandings about labor obligations that will be repaid
in time. These obligations are to be repaid in similar labor services or goods.
When people receive help in time of need, they know they are obligated to
return the service when the donor's time of need comes. One "calls in ayni"
when one needs generosity reciprocated, such as re-thatching a roof before
the rains come. At Timoteo CCarita's wedding to Benita in Pitumarka,
handwoven alpaca sacks were heaped high, stuffed full of choice potatoes
cultivated and harvested by the labor of the donors. These sacks counted as
ayni returned to Timoteo for his years of providing gifts of potatoes at the
donors' weddings. All of these gifts were the product of Quechua labor
rather than purchased with money.

One morning at Maria's house, I witnessed ayni when I went outside
and saw her ayllu neighbors on the storage roof with the thatched roof
removed. Some neighbors were making bundles of thatched grasses on the

Gathering of Quechua men and women at local market in Ccatca en route to Ocongate.

ground while I could see my compadre Eloy up on the roof's wooden skeletal structure with all the old thatching tossed below.

Eloy later explained to me how this was a day of ayni when the roof would be completely replaced by nightfall so that the foodstuffs inside would not be in danger of freezing due to overnight exposure. He had helped the ayllu neighbors last year, so this day when he called in ayni, they returned their labor in the same form, a gift for a gift. Eloy and Maria were obligated to give them chicha throughout the day and then at the completion of the task, when all sat admiring the new roof, a meal was graciously provided according to the unwritten rules of ayni.

Reciprocity is a way of life in the Andes. Institutionalized reciprocity has existed since the Inca empire used cloth and other status gifts to solidify relations with distant and ethnically diverse peoples that they wished to incorporate into the empire. While the state collected tribute of food, weavings, and other taxes paid in tangible goods by the population, in return the state redistributed land, foodstuffs, and other resources in times of drought and hardship, and as gifts. While cloth was one of the greatest signs of status and prestige, labor or the potential for work was also considered one of the most valuable possessions a human being had. Tax and tribute were paid by labor. Textiles, the fruits of weaving labor, were also paid as tribute and were considered the most sought-after gifts in the Inca empire. Feathered cloaks, elaborate tunics with tocapu designs, other finely woven

textiles, tightly woven *chuspa* bags (small rectangular bags specifically made for carrying and exchanging coca leaves), and belts continue to be prized gifts among Quechua people.

Quechuas talk, joke, and often sing together as they labor. Understanding a people or entering their way of viewing the world requires comprehension of the nuances of their native tongue, in this case the Quechua language spoken continuously since Inca times. Cultures live in and through the languages they speak. Languages are made up of rich symbolic units of sounds encoded with

Two Quechua men conversing at pilgrimage of Qoyllur Rit'i.

meaning. Translation of text or oral narrative by a nonnative speaker can alter the original intent of the storyteller or speaker; so understanding and speaking with Maria and her family along with other Quechua people on some level was critical to grasping the multileveled meanings of their conversations and intentions. Glottonation or higher pitch might signal subtle differences in meaning. Codes embedded in language are clues to what Quechuas naturally understand among themselves and to the multiple meanings in the spoken language.

Quechua was the official language for the administration and organization of the Inca empire known at the time as Tahuantinsuyo. In the Quechua language, the original word for the language itself was *runasimi* or literally, the tongue of the people or humankind.

The two largest linguistic groups surviving from ancient times in Peru and Bolivia are Quechua and Aymara. Quechua was imposed as the language of all state business and interactions with groups incorporated into the Inca empire, thus resulting in many dialects of the Quechua language.

Fields of tall, wild *ichu* (*ischu*) grasses in the Pitumarka Valley.

The variation spoken in Ecuador is called Quichua today. Carpenter estimated in 1992 that between 10 million and 13 million people spoke Quechua. Quechua is said to be the most widely spoken indigenous language in the Americas today (Carpenter 1992:116), even though it was a nonwritten language prior to the Spanish conquest.

While Aymara is dominant in Bolivia and Quechua spoken more widely in Peru, pockets of linguistic exceptions exist in each country. For instance, in Charasani, where Bastien (1978) conducted research, and on Taquile Island, Lake Titicaca, indigenous people speak Quechua, but are surrounded by communities of Aymara speakers. According to post-Conquest texts by Padre Bernabé Cobo, who lived in Cuzco from 1609 to 1613, the Incas sent loyalist groups of *mitamaes* or colonizers to live among communities recently incorporated by the Inca into the Inca empire. The mitamaes were transferred to new lands similar to their home communities to become a permanent part of that community. They were told to follow the practices of the local people but to retain their own identity through the dress, emblems, and symbols of their home region. The Inca nobility expected all nations of the kingdom to learn the language of Cuzco, and thus Quechua was used throughout Peru. (Cobo 1983:190) Clearly, the spread of the Inca worldview to new areas was a primary concern for political, religious, and social reasons.

When the Spanish priests and chroniclers attempted to learn and translate Quechua into a written text, they were especially eager to translate the Bible into Quechua but it was a difficult process because they had never heard some of the sounds before. In an unwritten language, sound and pronunciation are major sources of information. The language is constructed with the use of many suffixes to compound meanings or modify the root words. Forms of language construction establish an aesthetic of exact ordering based on the relationships of individual units to the whole. In this way, the structure of the Quechua language could lend potentially valuable clues to the decoding of meaningful structures in textiles as a direct model for meaning through rules of placement, and could be applicable to the Inca tocapu as described earlier.

Words have multiple meanings and interpretations leading to varied interpretations and levels of communication. Meanings may relate to one another, such as the word "*pallay,*" which means to pick up yarn and to pick up or collect fruit. Establishing the relationships between different meanings for other words is more difficult, such as Pachamama, with its dual meanings of Mother Earth and space-time. Clues for understanding the Quechua worldview must certainly exist within those relationships.

Spoken Quechua has a poetic, song-like quality to it, and Quechua poetry resembles Japanese haiku in its ability to express ideas clearly about nature. Articulate verbal expression is done with the same sensitivity, as are artistic creations of textiles. In Western aesthetics, textiles and poetry are not related art forms, but in Quechua aesthetics they are considered connected forms, as both are expressions of the same dynamic world. They speak verbally of the *ichu* (also *ischu*; tall, native grasses of the puna) weeping with moisture while recreating the shimmer of light on water by the meticulous application of sequins on lake patterns to create a parallel metaphor of light on lake water. Quechuas' relationships to the land, and to animals, plants, each other, and objects are expressed in their poetry. Poets in all cultures share a desire to weave words eloquently, but Quechua poetry is a vivid expression of the harshness, loneliness, and the exquisite beauty of the natural world to which they are intimately connected.

The Ischu Is Weeping

The rain falls on the hills,
it leaves frost on the tall grasses.
The rain passes, the wind shakes,
from the ischu the water drops
the clean water drops
The ischu is weeping!
Ay, like eyes weep in another's town!
They weep, the eyes, like the ischu weeps
when the rain passes and the wind blows.
When the wind blows the ischu is bowed down,
the tall ischu of the hills is bowed down
when the wind blows.
Ay, like the heart is bowed down in another's town
like the tall ischu when the wind blows!

Collected and translated by José María Arguedas
from Quechua to Spanish, translated from Spanish
to English by Ruth W. Stephan (1957:60)

José María Arguedas (1911–1969), well-known Peruvian poet, translator, and anthropologist, wrote about Quechua poetry and songs. He was born in the highlands of Peru but not of Quechua bloodlines. He became intimately familiar with indigenous ways because Quechua-speaking Indian women working in his stepmother's kitchen raised him. As an adult, he became one of Peru's most respected translators of Quechua to Spanish and eventually his work was translated into English. By observation and notation of their rites and customs, he collected music and folklore by writing down Quechua songs and poetry previously known only through oral tradition. "It is in the songs," he said, "that the truest clue to the Quechua nature is found. In them, the Indian speaks for himself, from his heart." (Arguedas, cited in Stephan 1957:119)

The iridescent, emerald-white-chested, Peruvian hummingbird. (Photo courtesy of the Hummingbird Society)

Emerald Hummingbird

Oh Sun, oh Moon, shed light on my road!

Do not sink so early, Sun, shed light yet.

Be a little late, Moon,

my destination is far, I am afraid of the dark.

Emerald hummingbird, hide your golden wings

do not keep me, emerald hummingbird

like the dove that has lost its young,

she is looking for me, my mother.

Oh cilili, cilili, beautiful flower!

now you see how I weep, crying out like the rivers,

like the winds, ay cilili, beautiful flower!

Collected and translated by José María Arguedas
from Quechua to Spanish, translated from Spanish
to English by Ruth W. Stephan (1957:57)

Young woman from Kilita wearing
naturally dyed lliclla, Pitumarka Valley.

Few scholars have been able to translate Quechua with the same sensitivity that it has in the original words. In the introduction to *The Singing
Mountaineers* (Stephan 1957:xi), John Murra said of José María Arguedas's
writings and translations: "This immediately differentiates Arguedas from
other indigenous writers of Mexico, Ecuador or his own country. He not
only knew Quechua well and had an emotional commitment to it and its
speakers, but unlike the other pro-indigenous novelists, he was also aware
of its literary potential." Arguedas commented, "We Quechua speakers
know very well that Quechua and Aymara are languages with vast expressive
possibilities." Murra stated, "[H]ow Arguedas tried to transmit to the reader
of Spanish not only a compassion for the oppressed, but a sense that the
latter [Quechua] also had a perception, a world view of their own, in
which people, mountains, animals, the rain, truth and all had dimensions
of their own, powerful relevant and utterly unlike the Iberian ones. He
took the very ways of phrasing sentences for which Andean speakers of
Spanish are mocked and used them in his fiction so that their outlandishness,
their incorrectness, conveys to the middle class reader of Spanish that he is
missing another cultural context."

"When highlanders speak Spanish, they do so on Quechua grammatical
underpinnings. It is not a matter of a surviving vocabulary, but of sentence
structure; even when every word is Spanish, these have been rearranged
according to the rules of Quechua, of which the speaker is usually unaware,
since the Andean mother tongues are not taught in the primary schools."
(Murra 1978:xi) Arguedas (1978) sought to express the soul of the Quechua
through their spoken language to a literary readership requiring a translation of Quechua culture as well as words. I am reminded of when Maria's
son, my compadre Eloy, said with tremendous pride, "We are Quechuas—
that is what we speak—here in Pacchanta."

What I believe he meant is that the people in Pacchanta express
themselves best in Quechua. Other Andeanists have recorded similar
insights, such as "their songs, beautiful in their own right, also articulate
indigenous cultural values and allow us to enter their world." (Harrison
1989:4)

Certainly they are a singing people, these mountaineers. The
young men and women sing as they walk, swinging, down the
mountain paths to market and church on Sunday mornings, and all
ages sing as they work in the fields. When several are plowing together,

they move in unison, leaning on their tools, pushing, digging, to the rhythm of their song and the work is done with amazing grace. [Arguedas, cited in Stephan 1957:12–13]

Through study of the multiple meanings for particular words and the relationships of the parts of Quechua speech and now as a written language, one can approach an understanding of the diversity of their metaphor and humor. The warmth of the people as well as respect for their ancestors comes through their laughter and jokes. It is a language of onomatopoeia where sound and meaning are one. The qualities of a guttural language with slight changes in clicking, pauses, silences, and breath during speech communicate fine variations of meaning. The juxtaposition of syllables and suffixes emphasizes the importance of meaning through sound to Quechua thought and worldview.

Sometimes in a high Andean valley, a condor overhead or a lost llama is heard and echoed before it is seen. The sense of hearing is as important as sight, as are taste, touch, and smell. Sensory perception is more equally balanced among the Quechua than in Western culture, which is more sight oriented, especially in the use of the printed word. Visual forms are used to express ancestral Quechua ideas, but in a more metaphoric sense rather than through the use of a written alphabet. Concepts are placed into woven symbols in what might be called visual metaphors parallel to the manner that verbal metaphors express rich ideas about the nature of life in oral tradition.

The Andean condor in flight.

Quechua Daily Life

In Pacchanta, on the day after the September full moon, everyone goes into the fields to plant. New *chakitajllas*, traditional Andean foot plows, have been made by hand or repaired in recent days. Smoothly peeled logs were fitted with a pointed metal piece and then securely tied with handmade leather straps. On the day prior to planting, large quantities of llama dung were collected in the upper pastures apart from the dried dung harvested earlier for cooking fuel. This dung is specifically gathered for fertilizing the Pachamama during potato planting. So begins the month-long process of potato planting all over the Andes in September and October. Planting time is coordinated with the phase of the moon in the late dry season as described in the Spanish chronicles by Garcilaso de la Vega.

Time has long been measured by moon cycles related to the wet/dry season, but the relationship of the sun to the landscape is yet another sign of these calculations. The horizon line is not usually level, but rather a set of identifiable peaks and deep indentations against a night or dawn sky. Landscape then is believed to be sacred not only for its fertility but also in its role of providing a method for measurement of the passage of time. Archaeoastronomer Anthony Aveni (1992:57) states that, "Cuzco's time axis commenced the planting season, signaled by the passing of the setting sun across a series of pillars erected on the horizon." Many indigenous peoples worldwide share the concept of sacred geography and the idea of the measurement of time by the relation of the sun and moon's rising and setting points displayed against landmarks. Fajada Butte in Chaco Canyon, New Mexico, is an example of this.

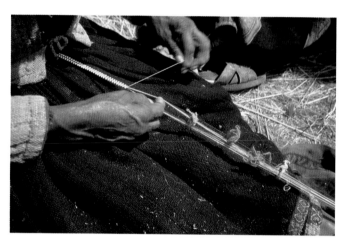

Hands of Manuela (Maria's mother) at work making *sanqapa,* Pacchanta.

During planting time, the Pachamama's fertility is strengthened by the combination of men and women working together forming a male/female duality. Males do the actual digging or "opening" of the earth and females insert the seed into the ground. The duties of males and females during planting are defined by gender but this is also true for herding and weaving. Women and children tend herds with the help of the family dogs as assistants as they move animals to higher grazing pastures in the dry period and nearer their communities in the wet season. While women weave the fine textiles, men are knitters in some communities. Men also make ropes and weave the coarser *bayeta* sheep-wool cloth for pants and *polleras* (very full, gathered, knee-length, Spanish-influence skirts), but more often the women are the caretakers of the communities' design repertoire related to mythology and are responsible for teaching it to the children. For instance, men have an understanding of the Quechua names for weaving designs in Pacchanta, but they defer to the older women weavers if there is disagreement.

Quechua people's hands rarely stop moving throughout the day. When they walk across landscapes bearing loads inside woven carrying cloths called *mantas* or *kaypinas,* their hands are constantly spinning yarn from fleece on a wooden staff with a weighted whorl or drop spindle.

Everyone spins alpaca and sheep fibers into yarn on this wooden distaff about a foot in length with the name, known as the *puska* or *pushka,* derived from the spinning motion of the spindle. Women's hands stay busy cooking, embroidering details of designs on cloth, or throwing pebbles at the herd or whirling a sling to make a noise to move them. Work is still highly valued, a remnant of Inca virtue.

Quechua people do not live in houses as Westerners do. They distinguish between the verb *kawsay* (to exist) and *tiyay* (to reside inside). Their days are spent primarily outside working, walking, and resting in the natural world. Houses are used for shelter, storing goods, eating, and sleeping. They are a rugged, outdoors people, who are continually occupied with collecting water, gathering dung, weeding the crops, corralling the animals for safety at night, sitting at looms, or stomping moisture from potatoes to make chuño in the outside patios.

On a typical day, Quechua women are up before daybreak preparing the first meal of the day, a *caldo.* These hearty soups contain potatoes, chuño, or other tubers, and sometimes bits of meat, vegetables such as carrots or an onion, noodles, rice, and whatever else is available, and are seasoned with peppercorns or a bit of cilantro. Corn, carrots, onions, cabbage, and peppers are more readily available at lower elevations and they are a welcome dietary addition, possibly obtained by trade with passing vendors or by journeys to the sometimes-distant regional markets. The day starts, then, with a large hot bowl of caldo (refilled until one says "no more"); sometimes boiled potatoes; and a steamy *maté,* an herb plant tea, such as coca, chamomile, or *muñay,* a type of local mint.

The work of herding, farming, or weaving is a cyclical, seasonal set of duties dependent on the wet or dry weather. Quechuas seem to have internal nonverbal clocks joining them in a mutual understanding of what will be done on a particular day. Even though I understood their conversations, some days I was completely surprised that Maria had already gone to the high grazing lands or that a new roof was being constructed that day.

Cooking hearth inside Maria's house with guinea pig emerging from warm opening in enclosure made for the animals.

The day's second meal is usually between 3:00 and 5:00 P.M. augmented by potatoes cooked and eaten in the fields during harvest. Another type of earthen oven made from dirt clods called a *huatia* is constructed while digging up potatoes and all workers eat roasted potatoes at break time. The

Maria spinning yarn on a drop spindle as her niece Alejandrina watches.

second meal usually consists of another bowl of hot soup loaded with potatoes or chuño and other bowls loaded with more boiled potatoes, which they peel with their fingernails. The potato skins are often dropped on the earthen floor of the house for the guinea pigs that roam freely inside scavenging for food. Guinea pigs are Quechua garbage disposals with a diet supplemented by young, green barley stalks. They are not pets, nor are the hard-working herd dogs. Guinea pigs have warm hiding places, such as the hollow areas constructed for them near the cooking grill. When a wedding, festival, or baptism occurs, the fattest guinea pigs are roasted and seasoned with *huatanay,* an abundant local herb. They are considered a delicacy and a special dish to honor the recipient. Efficiency is valued even in the case of fire carefully ignited in the morning by blowing into a long tube or piece of bamboo on the embers of the night's smoldering dung coals.

After the late afternoon meal, depending on remaining sunlight and warmth, people sometimes go back outside for a bit more weaving or embroidery until the light is gone. At Maria's house, when the candle or makeshift kerosene lamp made by her son Eusavio was lit, everyone would say "good evening" to each other. Generally, they gathered for one last hot herbal tea or a hot grain drink of some kind before going to bed with the coming of darkness. Unless visitors were in the house, they got up with the sun and went to sleep with the night. Laziness was not an acceptable option.

At Maria's house, every day three generations of women sat together near the stove on sheepskins sharing preparation of meals and peeling the potatoes. I remember once when I returned with gifts from the United States including a potato peeler. That particular day six to eight women sat in front of Maria's house peeling potatoes with dull twelve-inch knives. When I offered up the gadget, they laughed and then went right on peeling as before. Only Eusavio Maria's second son, who is twenty-two years old and has worked away from the community in Puerto Maldonado driving a Volvo truck for a mining company, stepped forward to try the shiny new tool. With awkward thrusts, he mutilated the skin of a potato causing laughter, this time indicating a definite rejection of the inefficient instrument. The women could peel the thinnest layer of peeled skin off leaving the meat of the potato intact, a method much less wasteful than this foreign new device.

The concept of private or individual space within the family house is nonexistent. Furniture is minimal, consisting of a wooden table, and maybe a few shelves and a bench. *Bancos* or adobe platforms are built with mud-straw bricks, a building material used in New Mexico to construct similar benches attached to the walls. These platforms covered by animal pelts and woven blankets or textiles are the beds, chairs and all-purpose areas. The use of space is communal, with everyone sleeping together in the same room. The lack of a concept of personal space was clear when once during a party following a baptism, after dancing until midnight, I fell into the bed where I usually slept. Because the car battery and tape cassette for the music were in the same side room, people came in and out all night. Quiet finally came with sunrise at about 5:00 A.M. I was exhausted enough to sleep through it all with no care of who entered the room. Everyone had wanted to dance with the gringa godmother of Julio Caesar, Maria's grandson.

Young girl from Pacchanta during Qoyllur Rit'i pilgrimage.

Quechuas are not opposed to cleanliness according to Western aesthetics, but the coldness of the environment and their daily activities give them a different set of values related to cleanliness and body odors.

They work very hard and to stay well is critical. Young babies and children are bathed on warm days and then quickly wrapped up under blankets for a nap afterward. Quechua men and women tend to have thick strong hair because they do not wash it too often and never with detergents or manufactured soaps. Hair is not combed every day but rather straightened upon rising. Women have braids several feet long, while men have more recently cut their hair short depending on the village and preference. Maria's family

Woman's carrying cloth from Pacchanta
showing lakes with flowers inside.
(Photo by Pat Pollard)

never submerged their heads in an icy stream or even a bucket. Occasionally, the women unbraided their long hair, combed and untangled it, and then wet it and immediately rebraided it. Any hair that fell out during combing was carefully collected. In the past, women's braids were joined together on their backside by *trinzas* or narrow bands of superbly woven thin yarn but today many women buy trinzas of manufactured yarn for this purpose. Quechua women do not cut their hair after the initial rite of passage, the first haircutting signifying the child's initiation into personhood, which is as important as baptism in some communities. While adult women in the Ausangate region do not cut their hair, men's hair today is kept quite short.

Textiles continue to be a part of Quechua daily life from birth to death. Babies are wrapped with thick belts, covered with cloth and carried on their mother's backs in handwoven carrying cloths. Children as young as three to four years old learn to spin yarn. By the age of eight, girls learn to weave belts, and then more complicated textiles. Knowledge of motifs and ability to weave fine cloth increase a girl's status in the community. Quechua men knit their sons' first earflap hats, make ropes, and weave coarse blankets for the family. The entire family is involved in the making of textiles.

The distinctive women's daily dress from Pacchanta consists of graduated layers of skirts, waistcoat, lliclla and kaypina, ajotas, and montera hat.

CHAPTER FIVE

Local Clothing Styles, Looms, and Weaving Techniques

Clothing from Pacchanta and other villages near Ausangate are a distinctive but typical example of highland Quechua clothing. A person wearing these clothes would be identified as a Quechua and specifically from the north side of Ausangate peak.

Women's costumes include a *lliclla,* a small rectangular shoulder cloth sometimes worn in four or five layers for special occasions, often with the finest sequined textile as the outer layer. Under the llicllas, women wear wool jackets tied by a string closure and with front panels covered with white or occasionally golden buttons, ricrac, and sequins called a *hoyona.* They are elaborately adorned and commonly turned inside out for every-day use. Under the hoyona, women today wear tight-fitting synthetic sweaters in brilliant colors without bras, making breast-feeding very easy. The *kaypina,* a large, rectangular carrying cloth, is worn over the hoyona/lliclla combination and knotted in front so that a bundle can be supported on the back with a child or goods securely held inside, or it may be worn open and flat covering the back in the style held in the front by a *tupu* pin or large safety pin. Some weavers, such as Timoteo CCarita, say this is a style retained from the Incas. Women wear *polleras* made from *bayeta,* handwoven sheep wool, either purchased in the market or woven by the family. In the Pacchanta area and north side of Ausangate, a woman wears no less than three to four skirts daily in a graduated layer effect where the colorful trim called *puyto,* either handwoven or machine-made and purchased in local markets, shows on the bottom of each skirt. On special occasions such as the pilgrimage of Qoyllur Rit'i, a woman may wear as many as thirteen to fifteen of these

In Pacchanta, three to four skirts are worn daily and as many as thirteen to fifteen for special occasions such as weddings.

heavy layers of skirts. During special festive dances, women wear a type of belt tied around the waist known as *t'ika* (literally, flower), a cord with large, colorful, tied tassel bundles that are a sign she is single and available. At dances for baptisms, weddings, or other festive occasions, a woman's weight in beads and textiles is a sign of her attributes as a potential wife, assuming she is available.

Women's head coverings are known as *monteras,* flattish round bayeta hats (with a sturdy inside core of coiled grasses), decorated with gold or green fringe on the bayeta fabric that hangs over the edges. The hats are secured with delicately woven *sanqapa* straps adorned with white beads, and the more beads, the greater her status. She wears no underwear, which makes the process of urination simple. Women wear sandals made from recycled truck tires called *ajotas* (also *ajutas*). They use small rectangular cloths called unkunas for carrying food, coca, and other valuables. In Pacchanta, the layered skirts reveal the puyto with the layering effect. On the southeast side of Ausangate in Chilca and Pitumarka, the layered skirts are all the same length and slightly longer than skirts in Pacchanta. Another distinctive aspect of the Pitumarka costume is the diamond-shaped montera hat with no fringe, and some older hats contain shiny gold and silver threads to reflect the sunshine. Pitumarka Valley women wear fewer sequins and beads, while in Pacchanta they signify status. Small girls adopt the exact same costume shortly after they can walk and control bowel movements.

Men's attire in Pacchanta is more likely to contain manufactured items

from the local and Cuzco markets. Many young men in Pacchanta prefer brilliant blue, turquoise, or even red synthetic pants, while the older men still wear dark, wool, knee-length, handwoven bayeta pants with an underlayer of white bayeta sheep-wool knee pants. Knee-length pants are more practical for working in the fields and men wearing long pants often roll them up. Men's fine dress includes a sheep-wool jacket (hoyona) or vest (*chaleco*), also adorned with sequins, ricrac, and white buttons, similar to the women's hoyona. Distinctive parts of men's attire are the handwoven ponchos, which are embroidered on top with layers of white beads and sequins after the weaving is off the loom. The ponchos become quite heavy but the beads and sequins, like the llicllas, are metaphors for the shimmering of light on the glacier-fed highland lakes. Men wear T-shirts, sweaters, synthetic "Adidas" jackets, or cotton shirts under their ponchos. Some men have a work poncho and a fine adorned poncho similar to the less adorned ponchos in Pitumarka.

In Pitumarka, the men's daily costume includes a poncho, wool chullo or earflap hat, and as shown here the old style of two pairs of wool pants layered white underneath and dark on top (ABOVE, LEFT). In Pacchanta, men wear a brightly colored and adorned poncho topped by a beaded chullo hat with *t'ika* or flower tassels hanging down the back, but they often purchase their pants in the local market (ABOVE, RIGHT).

In Ausangate, a young boy, held to his mother's back in a kaypina cloth, wears his first beaded chullo made by his father.

Men also wear ajotas as standard, efficient Quechua footwear, because they are sturdy in wet conditions and in crossing rivers. While ajotas are a sign of indigenous identity in the *campo* (countryside), they identify the wearer as a *campesino* (peasant) when worn in the cities, where indigenous people suffer discrimination. Men make the knitted sheep-wool or alpaca earflap hats called *chullo*s. A male is rarely seen without his chullo from the time his father knits his first hat for him.

Young boys' hats are often ornately adorned with white beads and the large tassels called *t'ikas* or literally flowers hanging from each ear at the sides and down the back. If a man cannot knit, it is his responsibility to have a close male friend who is a good knitter make it for him. The chullos are elaborate in design and adornment. Men wear a felt hat over their chullos. The current trend is for men to wear their hair cut short while women's hair is braided and rarely cut. These felt hats are adorned with woven hatbands called *sentillo,* heavily loaded with white beads as a status marker. A man's head becomes quite colorful with the t'ika adornment peeking out from under his felt hat and the multiple strands of sentillo. The chullo is the last item of men's traditional clothing relinquished when a man conforms to outside standards. The poncho is the second most commonly used item of men's clothing, which provides warmth in cold climates and makes a strong statement of indigenous identity.

Men are rarely without their *chuspas,* which are finely woven and often

Unkuna and unkunita cloths are used for carrying coca and offerings. (Photo by Pat Pollard)

have a separate supplemental pocket for *llipta,* the lime ash catalyst that activates the alkaloids in coca. Quechua clothing lacks pockets and not all chuspas have these special small pockets. In contrast to Pacchanta and the north side of Ausangate, Chilca and Pitumarka men use less adornment on their ponchos or chullos and more naturally dyed yarn. An all-natural yarn textile made of sheep or alpaca fibers in their natural colors is called *qayto.* Men use a smaller cloth than an unkuna called an unkunita for sheltering offerings after they are prepared and before they are burned.

Like girls who adopt their mothers' clothing, boys proudly adopt the chullo and poncho that their fathers use. If they attend school, boys often also use a larger handwoven bag with traditional designs for carrying their books.

Some shapes of clothing today relate to past forms or styles of clothing that have survived centuries of continuous use. While they may have been adapted in some ways, the exact original Quechua words for the names date to Inca precedents (Cobo 1990:185–89) Interestingly, the women's lliclla is exactly the same word used by the Inca people for a woman's shoulder cloth. The term *wincha* still means a woman's headband (which are used in Charasani, Bolivia, but not in Pacchanta, although the word survives for this textile in both places); a tupu is still a fastening pin for kaypinas and lliclllas; an unkuna is still a rectangular cloth used to carry personal possessions and coca; and sandals are called ajotas, from the word *usuta* (fiber sandal). In contrast, Inca

Weaver working on her backstrap loom in Ccachin near Lares.

The technical apparatus of backstrap looms depicted in the drawings of Guamán Poma in the 1500s in Peru are structurally the same type of loom used by contemporary Quechua weavers to produce warp-face weaves in Ausangate and regions near Cuzco.

women wore an *anaku* (dress), *chiquira* (beads on the chest), *pampacona* (cloth head coverings), and shoulder cloths that were often left hanging open and flat across their backs.

Men's clothing that has retained the original Quechua names from the Inca horizon period are the chuspa bag for carrying coca and the unkunita for offerings. Inca men wore a *yacolla* (cloak), *guara* (loincloth), earplugs, and an *unku* (tunic). (Cobo 1990:185–89) The survival of some Inca clothing forms with their original Quechua names suggests a link to the ancient past, while the Spanish-introduced polleras and men's ankle-length trousers indicate the integration of new forms. Identity or expression of membership in particular communities is still a visual language of ethnicity. This identity works for rural Quechuas within their communities and against them when they enter the city where such clothing makes them the object of discrimination. They continue to appreciate finely made, homespun cloth from natural fibers produced on backstrap looms, and grant higher status to those who weave the finest.

Contemporary Andean weaving looms are of two types: the ancestral backstrap loom and the floor loom brought by Europeans to the Americas. The European loom is immobile and heavy, used primarily for blankets, wall hangings, and saddle blankets. In Pacchanta, as in most of the highland regions of Peru and Bolivia, the majority of the older-style textiles are warp-faced weaves created on horizontal backstrap looms with four stakes.

BACKSTRAP LOOM and WEAVING TOOLS

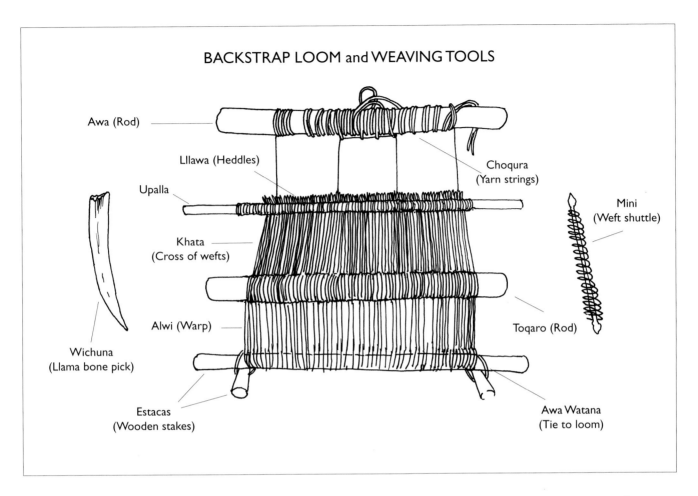

Awa (Rod)

Lllawa (Heddles)

Upalla

Khata
(Cross of wefts)

Alwi (Warp)

Wichuna
(Llama bone pick)

Estacas
(Wooden stakes)

Choqura
(Yarn strings)

Mini
(Weft shuttle)

Toqaro (Rod)

Awa Watana
(Tie to loom)

Drawing of backstrap loom, with Quechua names provided for parts by Timoteo CCarita. (Drawing courtesy of Maxwell Museum of Anthropology, University of New Mexico)

In contrast to the floor loom, this efficient loom has few parts and is portable. The same design for backstrap looms has been used continuously through pre-Inca and Inca eras as documented on Moche ceramics, carved gourds, and the chronicler Guamán Poma. The wooden pegs, rods, and shuttles remain the same materials as used previously, but today an occasional functional piece of PVC substitutes for the upper shed or a piece of rebar can be used for the ground stake.

The warp-faced weave technique is described by Ann Pollard Rowe (1977b:13) as follows: "[T]he warps (the vertical yarns stretched on the loom) are much more closely spaced than the wefts (the horizontal yarns) so that the weft does not show on either surface of the fabric . . . but passes between the two layers of warps which interchange to form the woven structure." This structure is necessary to make the complicated designs known as pallay, literally picked yarns, woven by Quechua women. The alternate weave called weft-faced occurs when the warp yarns function as the hidden structure for

Woman spinning on a drop spindle with her daughter near Ninaparayoq Lake.

the textile allowing the wefts to show, revealing both color and designs with no complicated pick-up techniques. Weft-faced weaving is usually done to make bayeta (or *bayta* as the word is pronounced in Pacchanta), the coarser fabric made for skirts, pants, men's carrying cloths, or functional llama-wool blankets, and in the past for men's shirts. Men customarily weave this bayeta fabric with no pallay or designs.

Quechua weaving is both social and communal. Aunts, daughters, grand-mothers, children, nieces, and cousins along with an occasional male visitor may be present when weaving is being done. Weavings at rest are rolled up and often left outside on the supporting stake structure so that when the weaver returns, she merely unrolls the loom, attaches the backstrap around her waist and begins to weave where she left off. Older weavers talk and joke as they weave and watch children, spending many hours each day at their looms in the dry season. Young girls often begin weaving on a toe or belt loom, practicing at first on smaller textiles such as bags or belts with no designs. In Pacchanta, as throughout the Andes, mothers teach their daughters to weave

Four of the twenty moneybags known as pachaq chaki comprising a sample set of local weaving designs used to stimulate conversations about local aesthetics and specific Quechua names. (Photo by Pat Pollard)

in the same way that they learned from their mothers, that is, the various designs of the community are taught in a particular order. One often hears younger girls counting the design pick-up arrangements in Quechua numbers. Clearly they are memorizing the mathematical relationships of the pattern.

As an outside apprentice, I learned in exactly the same order as the young girls who couldn't help but laugh hard at my first attempts. As an adult weaver new to these designs, I was handicapped by my not having been raised in a Quechua household and being around textiles since birth as any Quechua child is. As Julia Meyerson said in her book 'Tambo (1990), "[A]s we lived there, I gradually learned how to be a proper Quechua human being—learned the hard way, without the benefit of a Quechua childhood . . . I learned how to do the work a young Quechua woman must do and how to behave correctly."

Maria's entire family, including the males, were my teachers. The males helped by taking my drop spindle repeatedly from me to demonstrate the proper way to get a finer yarn as did the twelve-year-old girls and Maria's mother, Manuela. Manuela could take several strands of alpaca fiber stretched like a spider's wispy trail between her outstretched hands in front of her chest and spin them into the most delicate, fine yarn, much finer than machines could possibly create. Her eyesight was declining and her arthritis made her delight in my gift of aspirins each time I came back from the city, but her yarn never lessened in quality. My first day as an apprentice ended with me being humbled by constant laughter and my deep respect for their incredible weaving expertise. Silea, Maria's daughter, wove next to me. We started those days with them laughing at me. One day as I completed my third bag, Manuela said, "You really do like to weave, don't you?" Each outsider must also pass through his or her own rites of passage. After the baptism of her great grandson when I became his godmother, Manuela said, "[Y]ou are an *allin warmi*" (a good Quechua woman).

Like many other communities, in Pacchanta cultural beliefs are still transmitted by wearing and using specific textiles coded with ancestral symbols during ritual events and in everyday activities. According to Andean logic, weavers place Quechua knowledge that they want to reinforce or remember into cloth, that is, they use a woven form rather than a written one such as a book. The cloth is then used as garments to protect their bodies and to carry their babies, belongings, or food, alpaca fleece yet to be spun, and even sacred objects or offerings. As they dance or participate in festivals and ritual activities, they are like billboards reinforcing inherited beliefs. In the more remote areas such as Ausangate, weavers still actively participate in the transmission of cultural beliefs through cloth. I felt fortunate to sit side by side with Quechua weavers, to listen to teenage girls count design elements in Quechua, and to learn to spin on a drop spindle from a seventy-five-year-old Quechua grandmother.

In order to truly understand Quechua aesthetics, Quechua weavers must be asked to speak for themselves. When I decided to study the textiles of Ausangate and Maria agreed to let me weave with her ayllu, I knew that it was critical to encourage weavers' discussion of the visual symbols in their own textiles and to visually document the weavers through a photographic record. Clearly this expression must be recorded visually as well as verbally.

I collected a sample set of textiles from the area, and then visited families of weavers and asked them for Quechua names of the designs. In an effort to understand their aesthetics and system of valuation, I asked them which they liked the most or least and why. They were extremely cooperative and seemed to enjoy the collection of current, older, and rare designs not often seen today. I purposely included a bag that a weaver had constructed from a belt woven in another region called Qotobambas near the Apurimac River and another bag that was started as a hat and then turned into a money bag, which Maria continually called the equivalent of trash.

The sample consisted of twenty rectangular bags about three to four inches in width and about twelve inches in length, although size varied. The bags are called *pachaq chaki,* literally one hundred feet. They resembled the shape of a centipede. Originally this type of bag was made to safely carry large Peruvian coins. Today they are not made in many other areas, so the continued production of these distinctive bags is uniquely Pacchantan. The smaller dimensions of the bags made them easier to transport than larger textiles yet they contained capsules of design information in their variations. Whenever I brought the textiles out to show the families, people of all ages would gather around them and rather excited, open discussion followed. They discussed each specific design, naming it in Quechua. If any disagreement occurred, they asked the oldest woman there and accepted the name she used. I often sketched the designs with notations in their words. They related more to my rough sketches than my writing but did correct a name here and there. This clearly made sense since they choose to use graphic symbols rather than written words to represent their ideas. Occasionally today you see a weaver's family name or a date woven into the weaving but this is not

Maria learns to write her name with a
pencil while her daughter Silea and her
niece Mercedes watch.

typical. Their reactions to the sample set of textiles confirmed for me the
extent of their graphic rather than written orientation toward information.

One afternoon, the local schoolteacher came to visit Maria just in time
for the late meal of the day. Maria politely invited him to stay for the meal.
Afterward, he spoke to me in Spanish about my weaving and asked me to
teach Maria to write her name. Maria has a sharp mind for business and
her house is located next to the local hot springs where trekkers often camp
overnight on their last night of hiking around Apu Ausangate before returning
to Cuzco. Maria not only sells textiles to the groups but also sends her son
Eloy to the Tinqi Sunday market to buy Cuzqueña beer, which she sells them
to celebrate the end of their treks. The schoolteacher had been hassling her
to learn to sign her name for some time. When I gave Maria a notebook and
sharp pencil, everyone laughed as she attempted to copy her name, which I
had written out for her. Whenever I wove I muttered the Quechua word,
"*sasa,*" meaning difficult. As Maria moved the pencil, she said, "Weaving is
easy, this is sasa."

I thought to myself, weaving is sasa for me and writing is easy. This
conversation helped me understand how our cultural orientation in childhood sets up our life patterns. These patterns are certainly changeable, but
nonetheless they define what is sasa and what is not.

It was during this time of learning to weave pallay with Pacchantan
weavers that I came to realize the depth to which textiles and rituals are the
forms used there to record cultural concepts, not written books. In places

where oral tradition still predominates, writing and literacy have reached the villages but have not penetrated daily life. Quechua identity, unity, and the indigenous way of life are values taught within the family and the communities.

Learning to weave in Pacchanta is a process like any art form. A level of technical skill is necessary, such as the basics of how to warp a loom and how to keep an even tension on the loom by adjusting the pressure of your back against the backstrap in order to keep your edges even. The community judges girls and women by their technical expertise but also by their knowledge about pallay designs, both in terms of how many they know and which ones. Some designs are much harder to execute than others. When setting up the loom for warp-face construction, the yarns must be carefully counted as to number and color. If this is not done properly, it is impossible for the weaver to make the designs. The exact counting of supplemental warp strings in the setup is critical to the outcome and is a skill learned from the older women.

As weavers work to remember the designs, they must carefully select individual warp yarns by lifting them up with a *wichuna* pick tool made from a llama bone. By holding them above the basic structure of the weaving, these extra floats across the surface become the design in an intricate process requiring precision skills. The weaver must calculate by counting exactly where yarns need to be picked up to make reductions and additions or be able to visually "see" the design form without counting. The more experienced older weavers no longer count the individual yarns; instead they can visually judge the design as correct or incorrect. The weavings have "one face" or "two faces," depending on whether the designs are created simultaneously during the weaving process on both sides of the textile or have only one good side. Single-faced textiles have one finished side where the design can be "read," while two-faced or double-faced textiles have exact reversals of the pattern on both sides with only a variation of opposite

Weaver in Pitumarka working with a llama-bone pick or wichuna for pickup of design threads, Pitumarka.

Kaypina textile with diamond-shaped lake patterns with center and side-band designs in the Ccachin style while the central diamond patterns more closely resemble Calca or Ausangate. (Photos by Pat Pollard)

colors showing in the designs from one side to the other. Double-faced textiles are more difficult to make and are highly prized.

When I first arrived in Pacchanta and wanted to weave I was asked, "How many pallay do you know?" I did not know any Pacchanta pallay, so I had to prove my intent and claim to be a weaver by weaving. My first textile was a plain alpaca bag with no pallay at all, necessary as a first project so that I could become comfortable with the mechanics of their looms. After becoming proficient with plain weave by finishing my own bag for carrying coca, the next step was to learn the first pallay named *qenqo;* the second, *organo;* and the third, *huasca.* I continued weaving a number of bags to learn more pallay and gradually began to understand the deeper significance of the designs related to local mythology.

CHAPTER SIX

Metaphor and Myth in Weaving Symbols

Handicrafts belong to a world antedating the separation

of the useful and the beautiful. Such a separation is more

recent than is generally supposed. Many of the artifacts

that find their way into our museums and private collec-

tions once belonged to that world in which beauty was

not an isolated and autonomous value. . . . A utensil,

a talisman, a symbol: beauty was the aura surrounding

the object, the result—almost invariably an unintentional

one—of the secret relationship between its form and

its meaning. Form: the way in which a thing is made.

Meaning: the purpose for which it is made.

—Paz (1974:17)

In almost every textile that Ausangate weavers in the villages near Pacchanta and Pitumarka make, the core unit or design is a lake pallay in a diamond shape. A rich vocabulary exists for distinguishing different types of lakes and qualities of their surfaces and sizes. Through the process of collecting Quechua names for individual designs in Pacchanta and while trekking to other regions, I discovered that the word qocha or lake was used in all areas near Ausangate and also in Calca, Pisaq, Lares, Patacancha, Q'ero, Paucartambo, and even as far south as Carabaya. In Pacchanta, when I asked weavers why they weave these particular designs again and again, they answered me repeatedly, "Because this is the way it has always been done," "This is the way the ancestors did it," and "This is how we do it."

I slowly began to understand that a qocha is more than a lake as outsiders define or think about lakes. Quechua weavers understand that qochas are storehouses for sacred, life-sustaining waters, and they represent a part of the cyclical nature of water as mentioned in Inca mythology. The frequency of lake symbols was the clue about the connection of their designs to water mythology. Remember that storage was a virtue during the Inca horizon and, notably, Quechua people still store any item useful to them. Wastefulness is not part of their existence. Glacier-fed lakes above the valleys of Pacchanta and Pitumarka store waters melting directly from the top of Apu Ausangate. According to local beliefs, these high lakes are repositories of the most sacred water of all, which comes directly from the mountain spirits.

Markapata lliclla with series of lakes (sinku) at lower left and upper right, lake pattern with pica on upper left and corn in mid-lower right corner. (Photo by Pat Pollard)

While lake patterns have individual names, a design may become a more complex statement by the joining of several ideas or symbols into a composite pallay. For example, huasca *sarta* qocha represents the concept of huasca, a wide lake of a specific shape joined with the idea of sarta, a series of vertical lakes. The designs are thus able to express more detailed descriptions of the types of lakes and their qualities. Other lake terms are *sinku (sinko)* qocha, representing the kind of shimmering effect sunlight has on the surface of a lake, *rumpu* are long vertical lakes, and *rurun* refers to a variation of huasca and sinku but is distinctively different. Deeper information is revealed through the relationships.

Design names are modified by placement of descriptive words in front of the main noun, qocha, which specify the lake's shape, light, number, or relationship to other symbols. *Tawa inti* qocha describes the division of the primary lake into four lakes with suns in the middle of each, while simultaneously creating a cross on top of the original lake. The cross is a pre-Conquest symbol with many references, such as the Southern Cross constellation in the night sky. Four was an important number to the Incas, and was even part of the empire's name, Tahuantinsuyo, which indicated the joining together of four parts or *suyus* to make a greater whole informed by the use of *-ntin*. Size is indicated by words such as *hatun* qocha, an extremely large lake. Other symbols, including flower, sun, star, or rose, are placed inside the lake pattern to indicate composite ideas. Timoteo CCarita of Pitumarka told me that for him the flower inside the lake pattern is the potato flower; thus, the combination indicates the importance of the stored water to the growth of potato crops and the well-being of the people. Lake water and natural springs feed the rivers in the dry season when the rains do not come.

In the process of recording various names of pallay, variations in the pronunciation of certain names were noticeable. Finally, I realized that this problem was the same as the Spanish chroniclers had encountered when trying to write a historical record of the Inca empire. Not all letters of the Western alphabet exist in the Quechua language. For instance, the Spanish created the spelling for "ayllu," but the way it is pronounced by Quechuas is really more of an "a–j–u" sound. In spoken Quechua, a general tendency to soften sounds occurs. For instance, when I first heard the word "*chaska*" (star pallay) spoken by an older weaver, I heard "chacha." I later realized that the pallay was chaska.

Other pallay designs include *chili-chili,* referring to a plant and flower woven inside the qocha shape that has medicinal uses for the liver and kidneys and produces a red dye. (Timoteo CCarita and Eloy Turpo, conversations with author, Ausangate, Peru, 1996) Other popular flower (t'ika) and plant pallays used inside the qocha pallay are *rosas,* appreciated for their beauty, and *waycontay,* an herb used to season roasted guinea pig. Chaska pallay (star) and *inti* pallay (sun) are often placed inside the qocha. *Huacra* qocha is a half-lake design, usually on the side of a long line or in combination with other lake pallay. *Weisto* are half-lakes in a series of vertical complementary patterns. *Ñawpa* pallay refers to an older pattern used "before" or in the past, and is also placed inside a qocha.

The popular *pichincho* pallay (also pronounced *pinchincho* or *pinchinqo*) represented a local bird abundant in Pacchanta, and was never placed inside a qocha or used in composites. While birds including the condor are also

Woman's carrying cloth, a kaypina from Chilca, Upper Pitumarka Valley, shows a variety of natural yarns and dyes commonly referred to as qayto, whenever all natural materials are used. (Photos by Pat Pollard)

popular, the pichincho pallay depicts a mother bird standing with its baby or *wawa* close by while teaching the young bird to suck the nectar or juice of the rose up into its beak. Weavers answered my questions about the significance of this bird pallay, although to them its meaning was obvious—the pichincho pallay symbolizes the natural world and how a mother nurtures, teaches, and protects her child. Pichincho and huasca qocha are considered difficult pallay, but are learned by weavers early in their weaving education.

Names for other pallay used by men in knitting chullos include *alqo yupi* (dog's paws); *bandas,* diagonal half-diamonds; *listas,* lines of solid colors; *viscachas,* the Andean rodent that looks like a cross between a rabbit and a squirrel; *trigo,* wheat; *pampa,* large, open, solid-color areas; and a variety of smaller lakes and middle lakes. Footprints of llamas were also knitted into some chullos. Men knit their own chullos and their sons' first chullo. If a man cannot knit well, he must trade with a finer knitter than himself to obtain his son's hat. Knitting a high-quality hat may take as long as a month. Men could identify and name all the knit pallay and often could also name the woven pallay names, but women had greater expertise in the naming of weaving pallay.

In attempting to collect a finite number of pallay designs for the region, I found that the number of composite concepts could be infinite. I cannot report a finite number of pallay, but several weavers estimated that about forty are still known and used in Pacchanta. These include pallay names used to describe knitting motifs for chullos. I have indicated the individual names for lakes, but this research is open ended and will be continued as long as such fascinating word phrases such as "t'ika sarta chacha qocha" are heard, indicating composite ideas of lakes with vertical orientation, and flowers and stars inside. Collecting the names of pallay from contemporary weavers gives us a clue that weaving is a dynamic tradition, capable of incorporating changing influences and new ideas into a heritage of communication through cloth.

Composite metaphoric visual representation dates back to pre-Columbian use of composite figures. In Paracas textile designs, composite human-bird, animal, and fish combinations were used to express cultural values. (Paul 1990) Textile specialists have documented composite designs used in Paracas iconography. While Paracas textiles demonstrate a sense of intended meaning through the placement or relative positioning of symbols, contemporary Pacchantan textiles also use placement of symbols within symbols to indicate more complex meanings.

Placement and relative positioning of knots in the Inca quipu gave meaning to the knots representing numbers or number sets zero through nine, among other concepts. While these knots can be understood to represent a base ten through comprehension of the rules of placement, the same knots can represent numbers in the hundreds of thousands. When counting numbers in the Quechua language, the same logic works. One counts from one to nine but according to the rules of position and placement, what appears to be random repetition is an order with placeholders. For instance, *iskay chunka iskayoq* is the number twenty-two. The repetition of the word "iskay" appears asymmetrical and random without the code. "Iskay (two) chunka" means that two is in the ten's place. The second "iskay" has the suffix "yoq," meaning that two is in the one's place. Thus, two times ten and two times one equals twenty-two.

If these rules were applied to the apparent randomness of tocapu design, one might "read" the information like quipus. But we know that quipus were documented by Spanish writers to mean more than numbers; they were also recorded as mnemonic devices to aid the memory in the telling of long oral histories or narratives. Did the tocapu hold stories, dates, places, and events in fabric? Clearly, some clues to weaving symbology exist in the continued use of Quechua logic and language inherited from the ancestors nearly five hundred years after a conquest that tried to destroy all memory of the past worldview, language, and memory.

What is the relationship of meaning to language? Is it the meaning of words in isolation we want to understand, or the meanings of

Pichincho is a popular Pacchanta weaving design depicting a mother bird teaching her baby bird to suck the nectar from the rose flower.

whole sentences, or the messages conveyed by the way words and sentences are used in conversation? What is the relationship of meaning to thought? In other words, how do the conceptual categories labeled by cultural symbols get organized in the mind, and what can such organizations tell us about principles of human cognition? What is signified by the way the members of a society arrange themselves in space, or hold themselves while dancing, or sit down to eat? [Basso and Selby 1976]

Today, when rules of placement are applied to composite designs in weavings from Pacchanta and Pitumarka-Chilca, the meanings of the symbols are expanded from the nature of the basic unit. Was the language of the tocapu a secret language known to the women weavers with specialized knowledge who lived in the acllawasi, the House of the Chosen Women? Today in Pacchanta, the women are the holders of the meanings of the symbols. The men can articulate many of their meanings but except for an exceptional man such as Timoteo CCarita or Luis Pacsi, the women learn, know, and teach the meanings of woven pallay or designs. While Inca repetition in geometric design appears to involve a random ordering of symbolic units, the insistence of Inca order applied to every aspect of the empire, including the detailed accounting of stored warehouse goods, the telling of epic narrative oral histories by the quipucamayocs as recorded by the Spanish writers, and grand architectural projects organizing thousands of tribute workers, clearly supports the idea of order with meaning rather than a random arrangement.

The unkunita cloth is an example of meaning derived from the shape of the composition of the textile. The unkunita is rectangular, almost square at times, but the two sides are said to make a body. This duality comes together in the centerline, where the two separate pieces are stitched together at the *sonqo* or heart line. Around the edges of a variety of variously shaped textiles and some unkunitas is a protective trim called *ñawi* (eyes). The small tassels on the four corners of the unkunitas are *chaki*s (feet). Names are those of body parts, but they are assembled in an unusual arrangement, with four feet at the corners, for instance, and eyes watching the entire border.

Asymmetry is an intentional arrangement with a sense of balance and purpose. If we could discover the Rosetta stone for tocapu, it is likely that within this seeming randomness, the logic leading to the meaning would be divulged. Isolating the basic unit as Veronica Cereceda advised could lead to discerning the exact formula in Inca textile designs, tocapu, and ceramics, and with this the relationships among individual motif units that were intentionally repeated with slight variations in color or line.

Contemporary ethnographic research supplemented by a fine collection of Quechua textiles from Ausangate comprise the evidence prompting these questions about a continuity of logical patterns of thought and visual expression through time and are complemented by my ongoing investigations and conversations with weavers in Q'ero, the highlands of Pisaq, Ccachin, Patacancha, Qotobambas, Carabaya, Puno, Santo Tomas and Chumbivilcas, Vilcabamba, Markapata, and Pumachanka. For more detailed analysis, see Heckman (1997).

The Symbology of Water and Color in Inca Mythology

Research in Pacchanta and other areas on Quechua pallay led me to a deeper investigation of the meaning of lakes in Quechua mythology and the cyclical nature of water. Myths concerning the circulation of water are still told and believed today in the Andes. The Waruchiri myth states that the "black llama must drink the ocean waters to prevent the world from flooding." Guamán Poma (1980: 254–56) said that during the month of October, the Inca month dedicated to rituals of water, the Incas tied black llamas in the main plaza in Cuzco and gave them no drinking water in order to make them plead to Wiraqocha (also spelled Viraqocha) for the return of the waters. These black llamas most certainly represented the celestial Black Llama constellation that dips toward the horizon in the month of October and is said to drink the ocean (*mamaqocha*) waters. It then brings the water back up to the skies in the form of rains that fall on the land and collect as snow or water that is caught and stored in the lakes. (Randall 1990:19) The qocha, or storehouse of the sacred waters, is critical to this cycle of returning waters necessary for the continuation of highland crops, animals, and human life.

Detail of lliclla with multiple lakes in series and various sizes, Pacchanta. (Photos by Pat Pollard)

What the people of Ausangate continue to reproduce in their designs and wear in their clothing is a complex visual metaphor of Andean mythology linked to the natural world that has been expressed in one form or another since Inca times. Andean peoples continue to acknowledge the "dark constellations" or the black spaces as well as the bright stars in the night sky. They still verbalize this myth today and talk about the Black Llama constellation with its eyes linked to the Southern Cross. The observation of both light and dark night constellations leads us to an understanding and discussion of why color, shades, or variations in tints might have also indicated certain meanings.

Color communicates privileged information today as in the past. Much of the actual meanings of the ancient use of color were never documented. We know that the Andean quipu recorded statistics of animals, labor, stored food, crops, and textiles through color-coded categories, but with the Inca lacking written records coupled with little notation from the Spanish, research on color is limited.

Today it is known that weavers of intricate belts in Qotobambas (Apurimac) weave red into their belts to signify the male principle or the dry cycle of the agricultural year. In contrast, green signifies the female principle, or fertility, the wet, rainy cycle of the seasons. They combine these two colors but separate them with yellow, which is used like a mediator in the middle of the belt between red-male and green-female. The chronicles did record the deep-red *laut'a* headband identifying the Inka, an insignia of his role as head male leader of the kingdom, but they made no mention of the colors that his female counterpart, his sister-wife, wore. Did she wear green? Because the chroniclers did not realize the communicative role of color, any recording of their meanings was accidental. Could a combination of yellow, red, and green in tocapu have had meaning similar to the relationship of one color to the other used by the Apurimac weavers today? We may never know.

Guamán Poma, October, month of the Black Llama myth. Black Llamas were brought to the main plaza in Cuzco during the Inca month of October in an annual ritual to ask for abundant rains based on belief in the Black Llama myth.

The Incas had an elaborate color vocabulary, and undoubtedly the colors used in their ornamentation and rituals had symbolic value. Pachacuti Yamqui, for instance, said that the highest order of acllas were called yuraqcacllas (white acllas), while a middle-ranking order was called puka aclla (red acllas), and the lowest order yanaaclla (black acllas). Murua writes that spotted llamas were sacrificed to Thunder, brown llamas to Viracocha, and white llamas to the Sun. However, while the colors used in different rites by the Incas were often recorded by the chroniclers, their meanings, unfortunately were not. [Classen 1993b:72]

Contemporary evidence indicates that color may be used in unusual ways to facilitate healing and rebalancing the order of the Andean world. Some shamans from the jungle will not begin a healing ceremony until they

Inca mythology and contemporary local stories verify the continued belief in the cyclical nature of water from the mountains to the sea and its annual return to the mountains.

change into a white tunic or unku. Gow (1976:124) believed the color white was important in fertility and death rituals in Ausangate, that it symbolized rebirth or regeneration not limited to a mundane translation of purity or innocence.

The major color scheme symbolizing the Inca empire was the rainbow. The rainbow flag is still raised every Sunday over the main plaza in Cuzco as the official flag, next to the red-and-white one of Peru. On June 24, by law the rainbow flag flies from balconies all over Cuzco to celebrate Inti Raymi and the week of dances predeeding it. In many festivals, as in everyday life, contemporary use of color signifies meaning. The brilliant range of natural dyes documented by Lila O'Neal (1949:123–26) indicates that color may have played a very important symbolic role in expression of ancient Andean reality through textiles and other forms of visual record keeping.

The importance of asking contemporary Quechua people in their language about what they are doing regarding color, yarn, technique, or myth, rather than assuming they are losing their cultural values because they are incorporating materials from the "modern or outside world" into their weavings is clear. Aesthetic values of collectors and foreign weavers who have a disdain for chemical dyes, synthetics, and imported materials introduce values that do not acknowledge why Quechuas might be making certain color decisions. Such preconceptions do not lead to a better understanding of why Quechua weavers choose to use such materials as lime-green acrylic yarns.

It is worth repeating why Pacchantan weavers use sequins. Today in Pacchanta, sequins are used because they catch or reflect the sun. Ancient Chimu textiles used small squares or circles of gold and silver on garments to perhaps also catch or reflect the sun as one moved in ritual or while dancing. Manufactured ricrac represents the sacred zigzag or qenqo. Pacchantan textiles become heavy with white beads because the color white is highly prized. An old Kilita woman told me that they previously used multiple gold-colored buttons until they could no longer find them in the local markets, so now they use the white buttons instead to nearly cover the entire front surface of their jackets and sleeves.

Manufactured items are incorporated into Ausangate textiles and life through active decisions based on efficiency. When weavers around Apu Ausangate select synthetic yarns at markets and use chemical dyes, the choice is based on their desire for vibrant, lasting colors. Since it takes up to six months to make a poncho, followed by application of embroidery, beads, and sequins, they do not use synthetics merely to save time. Manufactured synthetic yarn is re-spun on drop spindles by weavers before it is used because the manufactured spin is perceived as ugly in local Quechua aesthetics. It is the color that has value.

Because of ancestral rules and local aesthetics about what constitutes highly valued textiles for use and not for sale to the outside world, it remains critically important to make these statements of the Quechua worldview with properly handspun yarn tightly woven into ancestral designs. Tradition is dynamic. Change in materials can be included without losing the significance of why making and wearing culturally coded clothing is important. If weavers ever stop making textiles in Ausangate, stop following the prescribed technical rules or stop speaking Quechua, then the Andean worldview could be in serious trouble.

As textile researchers and ethnographers, we need to re-analyze our attitudes by taking a serious look at what Quechua people have retained after 500 years of conquest rather than focusing on loss of culture according to Western aesthetic values. Perhaps we need to try harder to see through Quechua eyes and sensibilities. The declaration by some academics that attempts to understand and evaluate Quechua life through the people's experience and perspective constitute a romanticized view of Andean life represents a denial of reality for and about Quechuas. Their very perseverance for 500 years shows strength and endurance in a nonromantic, practical, everyday persistent way of life. They do incorporate useful items into their world but carrying a transistor radio to listen to the Cuzco radio station that broadcasts in Quechua does not mean that they have lost their religion or respect for their ancestors. The radio is used to receive messages from family or friends in Cuzco. Whoever hears a message tells the intended receiver.

The potential of making judgments based on an ethnocentric viewpoint is always a real danger. As foreigners from a heavily consumption-based society, we have a tendency to judge other people at home and abroad based on the quantity, not necessarily quality, of their material possessions. Credit cards, bank loans, and comfortable air-conditioned houses, which are often viewed as necessities in the Western world, are not necessarily what indigenous people want or need. The modern world has useful medicines but it also has introduced numerous diseases that can be relieved or cured only by modern medicine. How can indigenous people's lives help us to understand the mythological, spiritual, and political bankruptcies of the modern or post-modern world? Why are we so insistent on focusing on what they are giving up to become more like us? Or are they? Cloth is the equivalent of the canvas or the blank page through which Quechuas, like painters and writers elsewhere, creatively express who they are and what they believe to those who understand them.

Through the weavers' patience and persistence of perfectly executed pallays and forms, the people of Ausangate silently go on about what they have been doing for centuries. While city *mestizos* talk about how the highland people have lost their traditions, many Quechua highlanders are quietly resisting loss of their ancestral worldview by making more ponchos and llicllas at this very moment, preparing costumes for the next festival to portray of mythic legends, and planting potatoes in preparation for the rains that the Black Llama is busy sending back to the mountains.

RITUALS

ABOVE AND RIGHT: The Sinakara Valley under the glacier of Colque Cruz (Silver Cross), mythologically known as the silver gate or Colque Punku is the site of the annual sacred pilgrimage of El Señor de Qoyllur Rit'i in the Ausangate region.

PRECEEDING PAGE: Crowds of pilgrims and dancers in front of the Catholic church in the Sinakara valley during Qoyllur Rit'i

CHAPTER SEVEN

Public Rituals

Andean Religion, Pilgrimage, and Festivals

Rituals reveal values at their deepest levels. . . .

[M]en express in ritual what moves them most,

and since the form of expression is conventionalized

and obligatory, it is the values of the group

that are revealed. I see in the study of rituals

the key to an understanding of the essential

constitution of human societies.

—Wilson (1954:241)

In the annual sacred pilgrimage of Qoyllur Rit'i held near Ausangate, dancers wear their finest textiles incorporated into their costumes. Qoyllur Rit'i is not only the most important pilgrimage for Ausangate and Cuzco, it attracts pilgrims from elsewhere in Peru and from Bolivia.

Qoyllur Rit'i is a ritual of renewal through water. Participants express ancestral myths while dancing nonstop for days and nights in frigid temperatures, ending with some dancers standing all night on the sacred glacier. Textiles are a sacred, supportive part of all Andean rituals, and rituals are where remnants of pre-Conquest belief structures are the strongest. These events are living metaphors reenacted during festivals by elaborately costumed characters that portray a meeting of past and present worlds while acting out social struggles, legends, and mythology. While rituals provide powerful communal renewals, they also mark individuals' passage through different stages of life and death, all of which use specific finely made textiles when performing certain roles. Ritual specialists, whether Catholic priests or indigenous shamanic leaders, perform ceremonies on behalf of individuals and communities with cloth used as powerful symbols. Indigenous Andean religion based on animism has managed to survive contact with Catholicism, Evangelists, and Mormons.

The Contra dancers participate at Qoyllur Rit'i, Pentecost, Paucartambo, and other festivals.

When Quechua culture and language came into contact with European languages and traditions, a smoky filter of new practices clouded what existed. Former Quechua patterns of life, including religion, ritual, and art, became more difficult to distinguish from the new introductions. *Syncretism* occurs when two cultures or religions meet and merge into a single new form, as did animism and Catholicism, and Andean art and European art. Andean religion, deemed paganism by the conquerors, did not simply disappear; instead it is hidden within the symbols and practices of Catholicism. For example, Indian artisans trained in the Cuzco School style of painting, when commissioned to paint the Last Supper, painted roasted guinea pig as the main course. This enormous painting hangs in the Cathedral of Cuzco today. During confession when the faithful admitted they still had old idols, the priests demanded that they destroy these vestiges of the old ways, which they did but then made new ones to replace the destroyed images. Resistance often appeared to be passive, but perhaps this was because the punishment for nonconformity could be as severe as death.

> The intent of Spanish acculturation was to rupture the nexus between the objects, their designs and the cultural arena in which they operated. The signifying unity in Andean art between context, object and design was, by the late 16th century[,] under siege through the process of acculturation. [Cummins 1994:207]

The Qoyllur Rit'i pilgrimage powerfully represents the practice of how Andean images and principles meshed with Catholicism without totally losing their previous meanings for contemporary Quechuas. In the Ausangate area, beliefs in pre-Conquest Andean animism remain strong. Andean Catholicism is a different breed from the Catholicism of Europe; and while activities take place inside the church during the festival and pilgrimage, indigenous beliefs are just below the surface in the practices and symbols. Wildly masked creatures dramatize stories of cultural and class differences enacting ancient mythology through the participation of many dancers and dance groups or *comparsas,* including *chunchos,* inhabitants of the precivilized world who lived in the lowland jungles; ukukus, the mythological animals introduced into the rituals after the Spanish conquest; and the *majenos,* with their leather boots and whips who portray Spanish landholders.

Before the Spanish invasion, the puma, condor, snake, and camelid were strong metaphoric symbols of the Andean world. The Spanish conquest followed by the Catholic Inquisition joined forces of church and state in a major effort to kill the animistic spirit of the native religion associated with memories of Inca and pre-Inca symbols. Indigenous people stood before Catholic symbols of the cross and Jesus, understanding them in their own terms. During the Paucartambo festival, I asked a Quechua man near me about the Virgin of Carmen, and he replied, "She is Mamacha Carmen, the Earth, the Pachamama."

Chunchos dancers at Qoyllur Rit'i, adorned with macaw-feathered headdresses, portray mythological characters from the selva or jungle.

There is no religious system, ancient or recent, where one does not meet, under different forms, two religions, as it were side by side, which, though being united closely and mutually penetrating each other, do not cease, nevertheless, to be distinct. . . . [O]ne has spiritual beings as its objects, spirits, souls, geniuses, demons, divinities properly so called, animated and conscious agents like man, but distinguished from him, nevertheless, by the nature of their powers and especially by the peculiar characteristic that they do not affect the senses in the same way: ordinarily they are not visible to human eyes. This religion of spirit is called animism. [Durkheim 1954:64–65]

A fundamental belief underlying animism is that energy exists in all things—what we might call the life force—that needs to be maintained in a balanced state. When the energy becomes unbalanced, rituals are required to regain equilibrium.

The Indians of Peru were so idolatrous that they worshiped as Gods almost every kind of thing created. Actually, they made a glaring mistake by believing that there was only one Universal Creator of all things, to whom they always made their supplications and sacrifices. While at the same time worshiping, with equal reverence and with the same ceremonial services and subservience, second causes such as the sun, water, earth and many other things that they held to be divine. *In each case they believed that these things had the power to make or preserve what was necessary for human life. . . .* If they were mistaken in worshiping the second causes, it was because of the power the Indians attributed to these second causes to take part in the preservation of the universe. [Cobo 1990:6])

The Origin of Ritual: Wiraqocha, Water, and the Creation Myth

When the Spanish inquired about the name of the Andean God, the response was "Wiraqocha" (the source of all life), formed by adding "*wira,*" which means fat or foam of the sea, to qocha (lake, water) (González Holguín [1608] 1952:65). "Wiraqocha was the greatest god, the creator, a being without beginning or end, who created all the other supernatural beings, animals, men." (Rowe 1946:293) Q'on T'eqsi Wiraqocha traveled to Lake Titicaca from the ocean and metaphorically gave life to the rocks, caves, and the lakes along the way. According to Robert Randall (1987b:70), this concept clearly represented water, and the word "Wiraqocha" signified not only the sun and water but also the vital forces impregnating both. "The concept of Wiraqocha is the most difficult to understand because the Spanish tried to make it into an Andean equivalent of the Christian God and *they were susceptible to distortion.* Wiraqocha was an invisible god, a vital life force." (Randall 1987b:71)

"Wiraqocha was intimately associated with the sea, which was also seen as the substance from which all things were created. The sea was the source of water for all the lakes in the highlands, and so the largest lake in the Andes, Titicaca, was revered like the sea." (Sherbondy 1992:56) The Inca creation myth states that Wiraqocha created the sun, moon, stars, and all the ancestors from Lake Titicaca. In addition, the first Inca and his sister-wife emerged from the waters near the north end of the Island of the Sun. Through their myths, the Inca people were linked to lakes and caves as places of emergence, but especially to Lake Titicaca and the nearby ancient site of Tiwanaku.

V(w)iracocha, the creator[,] had caused the sun to emerge from the waters of Lake Titicaca. The first Inca Manco Capac and his sister-wife emerged from Lake Titicaca. Numerous Inca artifacts were found at Tiwanaku. . . . Viracocha came to Tiwanaku to fashion the primordial human race and animals from sacred lake clay. On the human models[,] Viracocha painted the different clothes and distinct costumes that would distinguish the many different ethnicities of the Andes, and each group was instructed in its different language and customs. The creator ordered the people to descend deep into the earth and mountains, and then to re-emerge separately from caves, springs, lakes and hills in different homelands. [Moseley 1992:13–14, 230]

Mamaqocha, the Quechua name for the mother of all lakes, refers to the ocean and Lake Titicaca, the site of the Inca origin myth.

Water is referred to repeatedly in Andean mythology, including the belief of the annual cyclical return of the waters from the Mother Sea to the highlands already mentioned in the Black Llama myth. Celestial water is even cited in references to the Milky Way as a mayu or celestial river across the sky. (Urton 1988) Other water myths indicate that the Incas believed the waters of the mamaqocha under the earth well up to form the lakes. Lakes feed the underground rivers that then carry lake water to the smaller lakes. These supply the rivers and streams, and thus the entire world is supplied by water. The Inca idea of circulation of water was specific: The origins and ends were in the sea and the sea underlies the entire earth as a source of world water. (Sherbondy 1992:57)

In Andean reality, water in the form of rain, rivers, lakes, snow, and ice is essential for the well-being of highland animals, crops, and humans. Ritual feeding of the Apus is a request to the mountain spirits to bestow their blessings of fertility and abundance on the crops, herds, and humans. Festivals are a time of celebration and prayers for renewal occurring on the basis of an annual calendar. Dates vary from one village to the next. Each village has its major festival where patron saints and its version of Jesus are honored along with the dispatching of prayers to the animistic mountain gods. The Qoyllur Rit'i pilgrimage, one of the most sacred renewal events of the Andean calendar, is dedicated to water and ice.

Musicians playing for the chuncho dancers at Qoyllur Rit'i wear their finest ponchos with large lake designs.

Qoyllur Rit'i: The Snow Star Pilgrimage

The past is recounted and that time and space relationship is critical to understanding indigenous myth as historical narrative. The myths and legends enacted and told and retold in festival and ritual in the Andes are a meshing of time and space. What is past is considered a living part of the present. In Andean society, the distinction between myth and history is of little value. Myth breaks into narratives that look like history. [Reeve 1988:20]

Thousands of pilgrims make the difficult journey every year to the Ausangate region to ask for miracles granted by El Señor de Qoyllur Rit'i. High up in the Vilcanota mountain range near Apu Ausangate at about 14,500 feet in the Sinakara Valley, a lonely but rather large Catholic church with a concrete platform exists.

Every year just before Corpus Christi in the Catholic calendar, the quiet valley, which is usually inhabited only by an occasional herder and grazing animals, is filled with fervent religious activity. According to Church history, a miracle occurred there in 1780; however, according to Quechua mythology, the pilgrimage has Inca roots. It marks the annual renewal and time of rejoicing when the Pleiades or Seven Sister stars reappear in the night sky of the Southern Hemisphere after their seasonal disappearance. (Randall 1982:40)

The official Catholic Church version tells the story of two young boys who became friends there, Mariano Mayta (a young Indian boy) and a *misti* (mestizo boy).

> The young misti provided Mariano with food and the llamas multiplied. Mariano's father wanted to buy the misti some new clothes so he took a scrap of the misti's poncho into Cuzco. In Cuzco he was told that only the Archbishop had such fine cloth, so he went to visit him. The Archbishop listened, then sent a Church commission to investigate why the boy had the cloth. The delegation was blinded by the radiance of the misti and when they tried to grab the boy he turned into a wooden crucifix. Mariano[,] thinking that the visitors had killed his friend[,] fell over dead and was buried under a rock next to the spot. [Randall 1982:40–41]

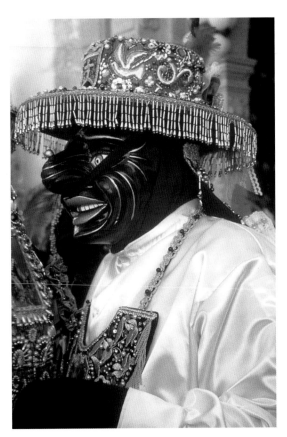

The dance group, Qhapac Negro, literally means the "rich blacks" representing the wealth of some coastal black Peruvians.

Today the Christ figure of El Señor de Qoyllur Rit'i is on the wooden crucifix inside the church except when taken outside for processions, and the popular Virgin of Fatima shrine is located on top of the abovementioned rock.

According to the Quechua version, when the Pleiades are not visible in the Southern Hemisphere for a period of about forty-five days each year, the world is a dangerous place caught in a time of illness and imbalance. Their return on or about June 9 announces the winter solstice and the beginning of a new year. (Randall 1987a; Zuidema 1981:3) In 1621, Padre Pablo José de Arriaga mentioned in his *Extirpation of Idolatry in Peru* (1968) that the date for Corpus Christi, which coincides with the weeklong celebration of Qoyllur Rit'i, was previously celebrated by the Incas as the fiesta of Oncoymita in honor of the Pleiades. Its purpose was the preservation of the cornfields. The Pleiades, he said, were known as Oncoy and were one of the main foci of native reverence. (Gow 1976:59; Randall 1987a:41) Oncoy in Quechua also means "illness" and the pilgrimage of Qoyllur Rit'i focuses on renewal of health and rejuvenation. "Qolquepunku, one of other Apus in the region of

Ausangate is said to watch over the health of the people." (Núñez del Prado, cited in Randall 1987a:43)

Pilgrims reach this isolated festival site under the glacier line of Qolquepunku, literally the silver gate, by walking along a narrow path uphill for three hours from the tiny roadside village of Mahuayani about one hour's drive beyond Ocongate, six to ten hours southeast of Cuzco. The length of the journey and degree of hardship depend on the state of the unpaved road. If it has rained recently, the heavy trucks sink into tire-rutted muddy patches requiring passengers to assist the drivers by pushing the vehicles, or if dry, there are choking torrents of dust. Vehicle accidents and traffic congestion on this dirt road linking Cuzco to Puerto Maldonado are common at this time of year. Most of the pilgrims arrive in packed truck beds or buses from Cuzco eight to ten hours after they started. Some community dance groups, however, walk for days, crossing high passes and following the valleys while carrying their cargo of costumes, food, and offerings on their backs. Throughout the Andes, distance is always discussed in terms of the number of hours it takes to make the journey on foot or in a truck and by natural landmarks passed en route.

After standing on the glacier all night, ukukus descend the mountain with large ice crosses or chunks that they are then permitted to cut because of their sacrifice.

Rituals begin with a transformation of time and space from the everyday to the sacred. Dancers facilitate this shift of reality by portraying people and mythological characters from different regions of Peru both past and present. The Qhapac Negro dancers (literally "rich blacks") represent the black Peruvian population from the coast and the north who have gained wealth, while the Qhapac Collas (literally "rich merchants") are from the South near Lake Titicaca and Bolivia. The chunchos, mythological beings from the jungle to the east, appear crowned with long, red and blue macaw tail feathers and chonta palm spears. Competition among groups takes place not only in the form of nonstop music by each band, but also costuming and adornment. The chunchos from the jungle, with costumes made mostly from natural materials, compete with the Qhapac Collas, who use scarves, beads, and sequins. The more elaborate or costly the costumes, the more validated the dancers feel. In contrast, the chunchos are supposed to be primal and this can only be displayed by careful costuming during ritual.

Among other costumed dancers, the ukukus (the supernatural bear-like creatures) in their shaggy masked costumes are able to travel the dangerous territory between earth and heaven. They converse with the gods when they stand all night on the glacier and then return to earth to live among humans.

In the Cuzco area, some believe that the ukukus are not bears, but rather represent llamas and alpacas, partly because the high-pitched sound made by the dancers when they blow across the rim of a small glass bottle sounds much like these animals. (Miguel Pacsi, conversations with author, Ausangate, Peru, 2001) In the dominant theory, however, ukukus are bears.

The ukukus provide a link of continuity between Cuzco and Qoyllur Rit'i as well as animism and Catholicism. On Tuesday morning after the main Catholic mass at Qoyllur Rit'i, they travel from the pilgrimage back to Cuzco to dance in the main plaza on Wednesday night. The Catholic observance of Corpus Christi follows the next day, Thursday, when all statues of the patron saints are taken outside from the churches in Cuzco on litters, carried in a similar manner to the Incas when they paraded their royal mummies centuries ago on litters around the same main plaza. The bear participates in both the animistic world and the world of Jesus or El Señor. Andeans do not have a problem with Jesus; they empathize with his suffering and feel he symbolizes justice. Their problems with Catholicism stem from the demands of the Church to give up their own ancestral relationships to the natural world of spirits.

After their night praying on the glacier, the ukukus gather on a hill above the church and large crowds to hold an organizational meeting for the next year, solve any differences they may have, and stand together in union before descending. They then make their way down, and dance in front of the church with the chunks of ice they have taken with the permission of the Apus as a blessing for having remained on the glacier all night. In the frigid climate of the glacier, death is not infrequent. Alfonso Ortiz told me that these mischievous characters reminded him of North American Pueblo clowns or tricksters in the manner that they tease pilgrims, play jokes, demand your tamale or bread, and act as ritual police.

The ukukus hold dolls in their own images in front of their bodies and speak with falsetto voices to make their requests or reprimand people who misbehave or abuse the rules of this pilgrimage, such as drinking alcoholic beverages.

Ritual serves the people as a venue to display faith, to realign the social

The ukuku dancer carries a doll in his own likeness through which he speaks in a falsetto voice requesting favors from the onlookers.

Dancers dance all night and day for El
Señor de Qoyllur Rit'i.

world, and vent hostilities, while at the same time affirming and renewing
beliefs. As my Cuzco compadre Andres said to me, "Mama, this makes
fifteen years of going to Qoyllur Rit'i. I will go for the rest of my life and
take my family. For us, it is the highlight of the year." Andres has worked as
a bellboy at a large Cuzco hotel for twenty years. For a Quechua man from
the mountains who has moved his family to Cuzco, his pay is considered
very good according to his social status, but ritual sustains his life. Andres
and his wife moved to the city when his parents died, leaving too little land
to sustain all his brothers and sisters. Their three children are intelligent and
excel in school. Through his devotion to his family and his religious zeal for
both Quechua and Catholic rites, his family's core is strong. Andres and his
family, like many other Quechuas and mestizos, sustain their beliefs while
living in the cities away from their natal communities through remembering
old legends and by their participation in religious activities.

Music at Qoyllur R'iti is heard throughout the valley by thousands of
pilgrims who stay up all night singing, dancing and trying to stay warm.

Vendors from Cuzco and Puno sell religious objects to pilgrims hoping for a miracle of money, good luck, mates, houses, good business, trucks, and the blessings of El Señor de Qoyllur Rit'i. After three pilgrimages, it is believed the pilgrim will receive a wished-for miracle.

Pilgrims sleep under blankets that they carry with them and pieces of bright blue plastic purchased on site. Rain and snow frequently occur. Besides pilgrims, there are tourists, merchants, food preparers, and arrieros who rent horses to people who are afflicted by the altitude and cannot walk or carry their belongings up the mountain. Pilgrims carry huge heavy crosses, elaborately decorated candles the height of a man, and covet their framed photos of El Señor de Qoyllur R'iti in their arms to be blessed and then taken back to their villages to help them every day in the next year.

Pilgrims take home other sacred reminders of their journey. After the ukukus descend from their all-night vigil with the Apu, the ice chunks they retrieve are melted into water. Pilgrims drink this sacred water blessed by the Apus. Through this pilgrimage and sacrifice, they are rejuvenated and renewed for the coming year. From the Qolquepunku glacier, the mountains drop off rapidly to the eastern jungle, thus linking the varied ecological worlds. After the ukukus' sacrifice of praying all night on the open glacier, the pilgrims below ascend to meet the returning bears and accompany them on their journey downward to the earthly realm. Some of the melted ice is placed in small bottles to be taken home to pilgrims' villages and for those who could not make the journey. Candles are lit inside the church before El Señor for relatives and others who could not come. Pilgrims devoutly believe that after they endure three pilgrimages to pray to El Señor de Qoyllur Rit'i and the Virgin of Fatima that their requests for miracles will be answered.

These prayers for miracles include new houses, Volvo trucks, procreant herds, stone corrals, good health, plentiful crops, and most recently, hard cash. Pilgrims gather small stones to build miniature houses complete with tiny corrals behind the Virgin's stone. These are visible prayers to ensure that the Virgin and El Señor understand what they need. Nowadays pilgrims may park a small, bright blue, plastic truck outside the corral to enhance their request. Women and girls bring partially completed miniature textiles to the Virgin to ask for her help in finishing their weavings.

Cuzco merchants and Aymara vendors from as far as Juliaca near Lake Titicaca provide objects to facilitate pilgrims' prayers, including fake miniature hundred-dollar bills; plastic trucks, four-wheel-drive vehicles, and sports cars; plastic shops; two-story houses; blank degree forms from universities and marriage certificates they will officially sign; good-luck amulets; palo santo incense; herbal remedies; tin milagros; suitcases bursting with paper money; candles; miniature passports with visas and bank checks for travel; crosses on chains; and most importantly, framed photos of El Señor printed with prayers. These merchants line the entry route like a flea market for pilgrims near the final station of the cross, inviting anyone to materialize their symbols for stronger prayers. Across the stream on the other hillside, merchants display acrylic yarn, mass-produced Lima-made clothing, knitted hats, wool blankets, and sheets of blue plastic, among other consumer goods. Qoyllur Rit'i has become commercialized but plastic does not decrease the religious fervor for El Señor.

Recently, attempts to commercialize Qoyllur Rit'i have increased. National and international film crews film the event hoping to capture the spirit. Several years ago, a rock concert by a Japanese musician with electronic equipment and generators failed as he attempted to use the scene as a backdrop for his performance. He unsuccessfully departed on horseback before Tuesday mass as ukukus were still descending from the mountain in half-frozen processions. The Cuzqueña beer brewery, one of Cuzco's primary industries, marketed a poster of an ukuku at Qoyllur Rit'i juxtapositioned with a bottle of Cuzqueña beer to advertise their product. Many participants were outraged because of the spiritual and ancestral ban on alcohol at Qoyllur Rit'i.

The Hermandad de Qoyllur Rit'i, literally the brotherhood, is a group of mestizo men dressed in business suits who carry religious banners but also have the responsibility of keeping the festival chaos somewhat orderly. They represent the regulatory body. In 1996, they instituted a new rule that no film crews could work at Qoyllur Rit'i without express permission from them, granted for a large sum of money in advance or an even more excessive amount on the spot. The new rule demanded that no commercials be filmed and no beer sold. The traditional ban on liquor had become lax prior to this incident; the special group of ukukus known as the *pablos* or *pauluchas* now more carefully patrol eating areas searching for vendors secretly selling beer to patrons. Patrons and vendors caught are dragged in front of El Señor and symbolically whipped for trying to illegally consume or sell beer. The Hermandad has tried to improve social services during Qoyllur Rit'i. A series of concrete restroom stalls were built recently but are too close to the river, and thus have contaminated the water for the people camped below. Potable water is available at several designated spigots and a small temporary medical clinic operates but few permanent structures exist. The Catholic Church sheltering El Señor de Qoyllur Rit'i grew from a small structure paid for by the pilgrims' offerings into a large edifice with a new concrete platform equipped with a booming loudspeaker the priests use for mass and announcements. Long lines of pilgrims wait for hours to enter the church, and then humbly remove their hats. They patiently guard the candles lit for loved ones, praying over them until they extinguish completely.

Qhapac Qolla dancers signify the rich merchants from the region of Lake Titicaca. They are an important dance group in Qoyllur Rit'i and Pentecost festivities every year.

Officials' voices screech praises over the loudspeaker for those who donate large amounts of money to the church and El Señor. Occasionally someone dies from exposure, illness, or a fall during Qoyllur Rit'i. Attempts are made to save the life of such persons, but if they die, their deaths are considered to be offerings to the gods.

The chaos occasionally calms but never stops. Dynamite explosions echo in the cold night air, which are considered means to speak even louder to the gods, as dark figures dance to bands simultaneously playing for their own dancers, interspersed with strings of ignited firecrackers going off at unpredictable times. Sound is a powerful deterrent to the *condenados* or spirits who try to steal souls. The blasts shake the valleys and glaciers, thundering back down on the ears and psyches of the participants.

The pilgrimage comprises a full week of activity with staggered entries by various players. All participants wear their finest clothing, and are identifiable by it. Food vendors and heavily loaded merchants arrive by Thursday or

Friday to set up. By Saturday, truckloads of participants arrive at the village of Mahuayani below and then trek three hours uphill playing music interspersed with prayer stops at the Stations of the Cross. Greater numbers of pilgrims arrive on Sunday, and more climb up the mountain path all day Monday. The sense of pilgrimage brings people of diverse ethnicities together in a curious friendliness. Indigenous Q'ero people often wait to descend into the Sinakara Valley until many have left on Tuesday afternoon or Wednesday when they arrive to perform their own ceremonies. They de-

A young dancer standing on the altar to light the inside of the village church at Hatun Qero during Corpus Christi. The community takes charge of the celebration; no priest is present.

part Wednesday night, making an all-night walk back to Hatun Q'ero to celebrate Thursday festivities that coincide with Corpus Christi.

The church door in Hatun Q'ero, which is rarely open, is unlocked on this particular occasion to permit entry to costumed dance characters who perform rituals with which Catholic Church elders could hardly identify and would probably call wildly pagan. The syncretism of Andean and Catholic religions does seem obvious at such times.

The grand finale of Qoyllur Rit'i is Tuesday morning when El Señor is taken outside the Catholic Church on a flower-adorned litter surrounded by colorful banners with Padre Antonio and other church officials walking near him. The great procession first moves slowly toward the Virgin of Fatima stone to salute her. El Señor is carried in a counterclockwise route accompanied by dancers as far as the last Station of the Cross, and then is returned to the church. Qoyllur R'iti has changed as rituals must (Robert Randall, conversations with author, Ollantaytambo, Peru, 1989), but the faithful, such as my compadre Andres, still bring their families every year. Plastic flowers, fake money, and long orations by the priests do not diminish their faith in the miracles of El Señor de Qoyllur R'iti nor their belief in the miraculous powers of his image on their family altar, whether Catholic, Inca, or a mixture of both.

Most pilgrims leave exhausted around 11:00 A.M. Tuesday after a brisk downhill walk to anxious truck and bus drivers waiting in Mahuayani who depart quickly in attempts to pass the police checkpoint in Ocongate before the whole plaza becomes jammed with vehicles. Another thousand or more dancers and devotees ascend single file up from the Sinakara Valley to a double pass over a difficult trail where they reassemble and stop to rest after a four-hour hike. In Yanacancha, participants dance in lines that crisscross

Qhapac Qolla dancers inside the church at Hatun Qero on the evening of Corpus Christi.

each other as they descend to the chapel where El Señor of Tayankani will rest with them. At about 9:30 but no later than 11:00 P.M., all the pilgrims begin the night walk as they wind around the valley's side up to another pass with grand vistas of Apu Ausangate illuminated by moonlight, and at one further *mirador* or outlook, the moon shines upon the entire Vilcanota range. Climbing over high rocky trails using no flashlights, walking only by moonlight, continues the penance. Groups take turns carrying the figure of El Señor de Tayankani on their shoulders.

This pilgrimage aspect is about the presence and power of Apu Ausangate in moonlight. It seems to be a moon ritual balanced with the sun ritual that comes in the morning. Inca rituals noted by the Spanish chroniclers focused on sun rituals more than moon observances. Even contemporary archaeologists, excepting current investigations by Lucy Salazar de Burger, rarely research moon rituals. Powerful night forces are unleashed and the cold is combated by constant movement. Around 4:00 A.M., the pilgrims come to a stop, and fall into blankets and sleeping bags.

At 6:00 A.M., dancers form a long line across a level high plateau oriented toward an even higher ridge. The moon is still visible overhead as all wait together for the sun. When the first rays strike, everyone drops to their knees with their hands extended upward to receive the sun in what seems to be an Inca form of ritual. Padre Antonio, the Catholic priest of Ocongate, also dropped to his knees with uplifted arms. Symbolic whippings take place to rid sinners of their sins before the image of El Señor de

A group of pilgrims in procession stop to pray as they begin the all-night walk to Tayankani with Ausangate in the distance.

Tayankani. Night ritually passes into the *paqarin,* the new dawn, derived from the Quechua verb *paqariy,* meaning to be born, spring, sprout, appear, or dawn. (Morató Peña 1997)

The dancers joyously proceed down a broad plain starting from two opposing corners so that they cross each other at the center point, then continue zigzagging down the slope. Dancers wait until all have crisscrossed to the bottom, and then they begin the final descent into the small village of Tayankani. Upon arrival at the Inca-style, stone enclosures, pilgrims wash and feast while waiting for the rest of the procession of El Señor of Tayankani to weave its way home to the church of Tayankani after his journey to Qoyllur Rit'i. Padre Antonio receives El Señor's safe homecoming with prayers. Later in the day, dancers and pilgrims leave Tayankani to climb one last pass before a steep dusty descent into Ocongate where completion is celebrated with beer. From the chaos and disorder of random dynamite blasts and battling bands, the night walk followed by the new day's dawn has renewed the world with an ordered tranquility. Symbolic textiles have accompanied every part of the pilgrimage as clothing, costumes, and bodily warmth, as well as the adornment for Jesus and the Virgin, banners, and coverings for the cross. Ponchos and llicllas identify the pilgrims' homes.

What cannot be expressed in everyday life has been challenged and brought into a freshly rebalanced world.

> One motive for going on pilgrimage is the feeling that a saint's shrine has a sort of hot line to the Almighty. One purifies oneself by penance and travel, then has one's prayers amplified by asking a saint at his own chief shrine to forward it directly to God. [Turner 1974:3]

Pilgrimage and Festivals as Forms of Resistance

"The social mask dissolves during the drunkenness of a fiesta." (Roe 1993:256) Pilgrimage and festivals function as a society's maintenance program for teaching values of past importance while also providing forms of resistance against imposed laws and policies instituted from outside the indigenous world. Ritual continually reconstitutes society by bringing past and present together in an altered state of consciousness or "liminal time," Victor Turner's (1969) name for the state of ritual that is betwixt and between what the initiate was and is becoming. Ritual makes the past a vital part of the present and past social precepts equally alive in the present and future. (Bawden 1996:143) The education of youth by their willing participation with family and ayllu members in rituals and festivals is paradoxical to the idea that the ritual cycle will die as indigenous youth move away to live in the cities and are influenced by global values. In Lauramarka, the former hacienda owner managed to end the festival cycle, but at present many young people want to dance every year and small children participate annually as ukukus and other characters. Such participation is essential to the continuation of Quechua culture. Is Quechua ritual weakened if a plastic truck is used to represent the pilgrim's request, the dancer wears sneakers instead of ajotas to stand all night on ice, or if an individual's wish for education is represented on a printed miniature diploma? Do the mountain gods or Jesus listen less closely or are the prayers less strong? "Rituals, in order to maintain their vital significance for a people, must also change in accordance with changes in society. Qoyllur Rit'i reflects the complex changes affecting Andean society." (Randall 1987a:49)

Festivals have become a time and venue in which social inequities not openly addressed by the larger society are acted out. They provide a tension release for Quechuas and some mestizos to vent their resentment accompanied by laughter in exposing social injustice brought about by a long history of conquest, colonialism, and modernism. The refusal to stop participating in festivals and rituals is a camouflaged statement of resistance against the imposed order without the consequence of being thrown in jail or severely punished. The distorted space-time of festivals, pilgrimage, and rituals provides a setting for acting out ancient values that some Quechuas refuse to forget. The conceptualization by some researchers of a seamless meshing of the worlds of conquerors and conquered is invalid—the conquered do not simply forget their past.

Layers of meaning are deeply entrenched in symbols of resistance within the existing social, artistic, and ritual structures by which people live their lives. It is easy to hide behind a misconception that these structures have disappeared, when in reality they are often hard to access by researchers. An overemphasis on analysis without "deep contextual data" (Geertz 1973:3–30) means that researchers are creating rather than telling the story of indigenous peoples. The humanistic approach commands us to more truthfully tell their story with us as the "others" in their lives. Earlier I mentioned that I would use examples from regions other than Ausangate. For the purpose of explaining the *cargo* system used to sustain Andean festival cycles and forms of resistance, a particular Pentecost festival in Ollantaytambo, Peru, is relevant.

Pentecost is the major annual festival for the town of Ollantaytambo in the Sacred Valley, approximately twenty-two miles from Cuzco. According to the Catholic calendar, it is the time when Jesus taught the people that the Holy Spirit is within each of them. For Quechua people who understand rocks, streams, mountains, trees, the wind, and the rain as having energy and vital living spirit, the idea of the Holy Spirit living inside of them is hardly novel. Pentecost is a Catholic observance that simultaneously reinforces Quechua beliefs and symbols. Randall (1982) argued that the word synergism did not convey the way these two belief systems co-exist. During ritual time, symbols may indicate entirely different understandings to different people. For instance, when a Catholic priest and an old Quechua woman pray to the black-skinned Jesus, El Señor de Los Temblores (Jesus of the Earthquakes), in the Central Cathedral of Cuzco, it is quite probable that their prayers are grounded on entirely different interpretations of El Señor.

Symbols are multivocal. They speak in different tongues to worshipers who come with varied cultural and religious orientations in life. While Catholicism brought the cross as a symbol of Jesus' sacrifice, the cross existed in pre-Conquest Inca philosophy as a way to divide time and space into four parts. It was also observed in the Southern Cross constellation in the Southern Hemisphere. Alfonso Ortiz pointed out that "culture refers to a system of historically derived meanings and conventional understandings embodied in symbols: meanings and understandings derive from the social order, which also serve to reinforce and perpetuate that social order." What then happens at the seams and edges where two religious and cultural systems collide? Does the culture of the conquered people give up and die or are the people able to use quiet deceit and the appearance of passivity to fool the dominators? When Catholic priests made Quechuas destroy their symbols of the past order of Inca beliefs, the people destroyed some symbols in front of the priest, confessed, and asked for forgiveness. History tells us that they then made new ones to replace the old ones until they were caught with them again.

The main characters and protagonists of the Chileno comparsa or dance group are El Doctor and the Maqta.

Resistance to conquest assumed many forms, including outward ones through the efforts of indigenous leaders such as Manco Inca and later Túpac Amaru, and inward ones through the efforts of individuals who refused to give up their beliefs while presenting a facade of the appearance of conformity to the new rules. In 1992, while some Europeans and North Americans celebrated 500 years since Columbus "discovered the Americas," some indigenous people in Canas, Ecuador, constructed a billboard that stated "Columbus *carajo,* 500 years of resistance."

During Pentecostal celebrations, colorful costumes consisting of both traditional textiles and modern market items transform some dance characters into figures capable of emitting anger held within for centuries. His head covered with a wig, long-nosed mask, and scarf atop his long-tailed coat, El Doctor, a lead character of the Chileno dance group, portrays the *hacendado,* the man of laws and books who is always reading the rules to others.

El Doctor uses the whip on indigenous people to make them conform to his rules but protects his legs by wearing high leather boots. Fabric made into costumes communicates where words are prohibited. The format of his costume allows him to symbolically act out his mythical character.

El Doctor is constantly at odds with a rebellious indigenous character who he whips again and again in matches that he often loses. He prances with book held high as he yells out the written words in a loud voice on some favorite subject. He lunges with a deep moan by chasing the *maqta* or the indigenous "*chollo,*" who frustrates him by outsmarting him continually in a never-ending struggle, much as in everyday reality. El Doctor's mask is white representing a Caucasian with a large black mole on the huge nose reminiscent of a protruding erect appendage pointing straight out at everyone watching.

The Auca Chileno dancers pause to dance in front of the Catholic church in Ollantaytambo.

El Doctor, with the help of his Chileno fellows who are dressed in heavy black boots, dark pants, ropes, tall white hats with rainbow ribbons, and white faces, rampages against the maqta. Chileno dancers move to a distinctive double-time rhythm accentuated by a dragging motion.

El Doctor whips the chollo who has stolen an animal and now holds only the tail. The chollo harasses El Doctor, adding tension to the situation. The dialog is primarily in Quechua so Quechua people laugh hard at the insults and jokes.

One of the more popular sequences in the entire festival in Ollantaytambo is staged Sunday afternoon. El Doctor and the maqta whip at each other until finally the Chilenos capture the maqta's foot in a lasso. They tie him with their rope lassos and pull him up into the plaza's largest tree, but he manages to escape yelling insults at El Doctor and the rest of the Chilenos. This hilarious episode is variously reenacted each year emphasizing through repetition the continued unfairness of the man of the law, the unkindness of the book of imposed rules to indigenous people, the past history of Quechuas dealing with hacendados, and bitter sentiments over the war between Peru and Chile (1879–1883).

From the moment a dancer goes behind the mask until its final removal after the last public performance, the dancers become the characters. Their gestures, motions, and identity constitute the mythical character. In festival, behind the costume and mask, they are metaphors: they are not like the character or representative of the character, but become the characters. Dancers forget themselves and move with others as a unit with a single purpose: to act out myth and fulfill what they have promised to El Señor and their community.

As the Auca Chileno masks and costumes are donned, the dancers become the characters they portray for the next five days.

Under the Mask

Sweat rivulets pour over my lips
forging deep gorge waterfalls off my chin.
Swollen eyes from marathon exhaustion
attempt to squint through the mask's eye slits.
El Doctor holds the scriptures through my hands;
his voice comes from my throat.
On this fifth day of Pentecost, I am El Doctor,
whipping the Chollo for his insolent behavior.
I am the authority of law and religion,
With my book in hand, I have powerful proof.
But this chollo insults and infuriates me
with his stupid Indian beliefs in nature.
The mask melts the individual into submission.
In ritual, we speak out communally;
we relieve our anger and humiliation.
Our ancestor's pride overwhelms our lives.
I am El Doctor, the tyrannical man of words.
My sweaty mask pushed into the dirt by the chollo.
Under the mask, I sweat with centuries of hidden pride.

—By Andrea M. Heckman REPRINTED WITH PERMISSION
OF THE AMERICAN ANTHROPOLOGY ASSOCIATION, FROM THE
Journal of Humanistic Anthropology 25, NO. 1 (JUNE 2000)

In festivals, the unspeakable is spoken. Roles are reversed: men are women, and those in control are treated like peasants. Participants are required to get drunk, neglect normal work, stay out all night, vent anger bottled up during the year, parody the Church and priest, laugh and then sob together, and play outrageous jokes on each other. Dancers are not allowed to hit each other, but aggression between comparsas or dance groups is expressed through harsh words and insults.

The burden of organizing a festival is supported by a system called the cargo. A comparsa includes the dancers, all their supporters and helpers, their families, and all former dancers. The sponsors of a particular comparsa accept this burden on their lives and savings when they agree to accept the responsibility for the coming year. A couple usually accepts the responsibility but it can be a single person with a stand-in counterpart. The entire extended family, friends, and ayllu of the cargo bearers commit to help through a process called *hurka*. The cargo bearers know they must organize cooks and chicha makers to feed dancers, get commitments to dance, pay for masks, and help dancers with their costumes. They must also make sure that enough food and alcohol and appropriate foods are ready for each particular day, secure a reliable band who knows the group's songs, and keep track of several hundred other minor organizational details. Young couples, after becoming married legally or by their consummation of a family by the births of children, are expected to accept cargos for political and religious gain. They observed festivals and cargo duties throughout their childhood, but as adults they know they will gain higher status in the community when they are ready with resources and energy to accept a cargo.

After a year of planning and finishing details on the costumes on Saturday morning, the festival in Ollantaytambo begins on Saturday afternoon. With practice sessions and sewing of sequins behind them, the group makes its first appearance in the public square. Throughout five days and four nights of revelry, the group is required to hold vigils at designated times, sometimes in the middle of a cold night, in front of El Señor de Choqekillka (also Choquekillka), Ollantaytambo's Jesus figure.

A Personal Story of Cargo

Normally, only community members from Ollantaytambo are asked to accept a cargo, but in 1998 my husband Ken O'Neil and I received the cargo for the Chileno dance group for Pentecost 1999. Our history with this community spans ten years, including the responsibility of being godparents to four children, two adults, and a store. We became godparents through the personal rites of baptism, first haircutting, and marriage, and I became the godmother of a store when Wendy Weeks asked me.

Wendy Weeks and her late husband Robert Randall came to Ollantaytambo nearly thirty years ago. Weary after several years of travel through Guatemala and Ecuador, they settled into the Albergue near the train station where both their sons Nathan and Joaquin were born. Their partners, James and Lindy Dirks, parented two girls there also. Over time, they became members of the community and in 1990 they were officially married in the church at Ollantaytambo and had the cargo for the Chileno dance group. They were respected members of the community and their sons were educated in the local schools before going to universities in the United States. Randall was a scholar of Quechua cosmology and language, well known and liked up and down the Patacancha Valley and in Cuzco. He passed away in November 1990. Wendy is an accomplished painter who continues her life in Ollantaytambo and without her, we could not have accepted the cargo. Her friendship and guidance, along with that of our god-children, allowed us as outsiders to the community to understand and act properly in the position we were honored to accept.

Auca Chileno hats stacked next to the demanda or wooden box with the image of El Señor de Choquekillka during a rest break.

As outsiders to an indigenous community of Quechua and mestizo insiders, we did not have the advantage of the knowledge that small children learn on a daily basis from their elders. We learned by trial and error. Andean reciprocity is at the heart of the festival from the moment of accepting the cargo on behalf of El Señor. Community members vocalize loudly in organizational meetings the importance of the customs and traditions of the community. Paradoxically, group interactions and social dynamics work to alter festival patterns and at the same time to maintain them. While festival patterns of behavior, the roles of the dancers, and the cargos of the dance groups can change every year, the primary leader of the event, the mayordomo central, changes every five years. In 1999, the Catholic Church, through the mandate of the village priest Padre José, also tried to initiate restraints on festival drinking, outspoken visual statements against authority, and fireworks. Andeans like loud noises at festival times and drinking both

Cuzqueña beer and the local corn beer, chicha, are annual occurrences during the celebration. The Chileno cargo we accepted is a dance group known for their outrageous choreography displaying indigenous resistance to authority through the re-telling of the war between Chile and Peru.

Our godchildren and friends, Hector and Maria Avellaneda, had been asking us for several years to accept the Chileno cargo, so when we finally said yes, the group formally invited us to be cargo bearers. We received the passing of the cargo and possession of the demanda on Pentecost Sunday 1998. The demanda is a carved wooden box with an upper back panel displaying a photo of El Señor de Choqekillka. The demanda was the primary symbol of our acting on his behalf for the good of the community and dance group.

Not being permanent residents, we returned to the community several times over the next year to host a dinner, buy trees, and then work with dancers to chop the wood and stack it to dry for fuel for all the group's meals. After the October visit, the dancers seemed to stop worrying whether we would be good carguyoqs.

The cargo experience catapulted us into local politics, the local sense of time, and continuing religious struggles with the Catholic Church. Juan Behar, the new mayordomo central, held the first official organizational meeting two weeks before the event. He arrived one hour late because of a Mother's Day celebration in a neighboring village. After lengthy salutations, he conducted a one-hour opinion session about the hour that the event would begin. Finally, a vote was taken and four hours later, we had accomplished very little. The contrast in our cultural concepts of time began here but did not end until the festival closed. Culturally, we were focused on the hour we were told while other participants were focused on the event. They seemed to be guided by a faith that all would happen "on time" because of the guidance and help of El Señor de Choquekillka. During the October dinner, the Chileno president, Andres, had asked if we would get married during the festival in the Catholic Church. Since we had consumed quantities of Cuzqueña beer, we said, "Sí." He said, "Van a casar, sí o sí? Are you going to get married, yes or yes?"

Laughingly, we said yes. Closer to May, we realized our mistake. Padre José wanted six documents, including birth, baptism, and confirmation, and we would have had to attend lessons about Catholicism. We knew we would not survive these sessions, even though Ken rattled off the Lord's Prayer in Latin and I practiced the Hail Mary around two hundred times. I am not Catholic but as this festival progressed, I had to believe all these recitations of prayers had helped us. After we donated fifty cement blocks to the church for building a new chapel wall, the priest released us and we were free from marriage plans that only complicated our cargo. Padre José is a conservative servant of the archbishop of Cuzco (influenced by Opus Dei) who was dispatched to Ollantaytambo to get the community shaped up after the last liberal and popular priest, Padre Miguel.

Cargo bearers solicit promises for help, animals, and dancers through an old social process known as hurka. With the demanda in hand, the easily identifiable Chileno hat on my head, and in the company of a group of our godchildren and comadres, Ken and I walked to neighbors near and far up the valley to ask for donations of guinea pigs, hens, potatoes, making chicha, pots, beer, working as cooks, servers of meals, and other things we needed for the Chilenos in the name of El Señor. We presented specially made round loaves of bread tiered in threes on an aluminum painted plate with a bit of beer, wine, liquor, or soft drink. Old women removed their hats while they kissed El Señor's picture on the demanda and promised us five guinea pigs and two hens. The promises made months in advance are collected right before the festival. We drove Wendy's truck up the Patacancha Valley to ask for sacks of potatoes and sheep. We had more bread made in Cuzco to hurka friends there to bring cases of beer to Ollantaytambo during the festival. Beer requirements totaled about sixty cases of twenty-four bottles each, so help with purchases was appreciated, while many other donations are the products of work in the fields.

Pentecost always begins on a Saturday, yet the date is movable based on the Catholic calendar. As the day grew near final preparations required more time. We spent the entire month of May working with compadres and comadres, dancers, Wendy, and family members to complete the re-thatching of the Chileno dance house or headquarters

As the annual festival ends, this tired ukuku dancer finally rests.

for the group during the festival. We also had two cement bathrooms built since so many dignified guests from Cuzco were expected and the house had no toilets. After the walls were constructed, the plumber started figuring out how to bring the pipes into the enclosure. Finally the pink cement toilets were set in place, but they did not work. This was the Friday before the festival and pigs were still in a soggy mud hole in the courtyard.

Our sense of timing told us we were going to fail as carguyoqs and not be ready. But the pigs were removed, the mud was shoveled out and the hole began to dry, tables were brought in, jars of yellow and purple flowers adorned plastic tablecloths, and dancers began showing up to try on costumes. The toilets never quite worked right but the dancers finished dressing and the group with us in the lead headed for the main plaza to make a first entry into festival time and space. The plaza of commerce and buses was transformed into an arena of the sacred. Hearty soups and meals were served on borrowed porcelain plates to all visitors who came to the Chileno house, gallons and gallons of chicha were consumed, and dancers finished exhausted but content with us as carguyoqs.

The festival cargo system is invisible from afar. Knowledge is gained through active participation in daily and annual events. Support for festivals through the acceptance of a cargo is expected. Carguyoqs are recruited more often than drafted, but as difficult to avoid as a private rite of passage. It is a social obligation with great social rewards and devastating financial or material loss for a couple. The status gained outweighs the sacrifice of the give-away of labor, time, and wealth. Without the cargo system, Andean festivals would die. As in pilgrimage, the making of costumes, weavings and cloth along with other textile arts, such as basketry and sewing, accompany every aspect of the festival. Strainers for chicha are made of grasses, roofs are re-thatched, grounds swept with handmade brooms, and textiles constitute elements of almost every costume. Without cargos and cloth, there would be no festivals and without woven cloth, rites of passage would lose meaning.

CHAPTER EIGHT

Rites of Passage and Healing, Ritual Sacrifice, and Masked Identity

Rites of Passage

While pilgrimages and festivals are large publicly attended events, the progression of individuals through all stages of life is marked by rites of passage. Just as textiles help communicate meaning through the costumes and fine clothing of participants at large ceremonial gatherings, handwoven cloths embedded with symbols are central elements for rites of passage and sacred offerings to the mountain gods. The ritual exchange of *mama coca,* the sacred leaf grown on the eastern slopes of the Andes is an integral part of any rite or ceremonial event. Andean reciprocity is involved in both giving coca to one another and sharing the act of chewing it. Coca is correctly given from and received in a textile such as the special bag called a chuspa made for that purpose and for carrying one's coca, often with small pockets for llipta, the lime ash catalyst.

If a proper textile is not available, a woman will receive coca in the bayeta of her skirt and a man may even receive it in his hat. Altomisayoqs, the highest form of Andean ritual specialists such as Mariano Turpo, protect their coca in a chuspa made from the pelt of a baby alpaca, the softest of the fibers after vicuña. Their right to use the bag is a symbol of the position they have attained in life. Mariano and other misayoqs of all levels use the unkunita in ritual, which is a smaller rectangular cloth usually of natural alpaca yarn made in four sections and four colors, to guard the offering after it is made and until it is burned in the evening or night to be carried on the smoke to the mountain gods.

Women carry coca in an unkuna cloth and while they usually do not

Coca bags for carrying and ritually exchanging coca leaves.
TOP: Two coca bags from Markapata
BOTTOM: Bag from Hatun Qero with supplemental folded pouches to hold the llipta (Photos by Pat Pollard)

chew coca on a daily basis (excepting older women), they always share in the ritual exchange when invited, such as at weddings. Unkuna cloths are also used at a child's first haircutting under the plate that holds the scissors and to guard the child's snipped hair. Traditionally, the soon-to-be married is required to make cloth as gifts for her intended spouse. In some areas, women also weave the finest ponchos or llicllas or kaypinas with intertwined designs of duality within the pallay and are recognizable by the special design work. Fine handmade textiles traditionally accompany people throughout all aspects of life and stay with them into death and burial rituals.

First Haircutting

During the Inca era, *rutuy* (to cut the hair, also spelled *rutuyku* or *rutuchikuy)* or a child's first haircutting, was an occasion for gifts of silver, cloth, wool, and cotton given by participants to mark the passage of the baby into childhood. The infant mortality rate is high during the first year of life in the harsh, cold climate of the highlands. Severe bronchitis or dehydration can cause death. The first haircutting rite celebrates life. Those attending the ceremony donate money and clothing, and sometimes a sheep for the well-being of the child. In return, the family gives attendees food and drink, and everyone dances together in celebration. Usually this event occurs between one and four years of age. Great danger exists for the child's soul if death occurs before this rite.

The invited godparents-to-be ceremoniously ask the parents' permission to begin the haircutting rite. Taking the scissors, the *padrino* and madrina each cut a large piece of soft baby hair, carefully placing it on a plate with flowers if available. An unkuna cloth is placed under the plate, and the scissors rests on the plate between snips. Next, each godparent places a gift of money on the cut hair followed by the gracious shoulder-patting hug Andeans traditionally give one another from the parents and the ritual drink of Cuzqueña beer, locally made corn chicha, or a soft drink. Spectators become participants as each person present asks permission of the padrino and madrina for the privilege of cutting the child's hair next. Many young children are remarkably quiet, having a sense of the importance of what is transpiring. When all have had a chance to cut the hair, the godparents, again with pomp and ceremony, count the money and present it to the parents in a very formal manner, saying to all in the room that they entrust the parents to guard this amount of money for the child's future for some later need they may have. Celebratory drinking and dancing may continue until dawn.

During the first hair-cutting rite of passage, the baby becomes a child and the godparent accepts his or her responsibilities.

Courtship

A Quechua woman's desirability as a wife is increased by such practical qualities as being a fine weaver. Her ability to impress her spouse-to-be and his family with weaving is an asset in her search for a mate. Acceptable textile gifts often marks agreement for the union to take place. Baptisms, weddings, or village holidays and festivals are times when young single people available for courtship come dressed in extravagant displays of their family's finery. A circle dance with single males and females occurs or, as often happens, only a circle of young girls dance together with young men breaking in between two girls as they grab hands reforming the circle. A young man may take a woman out of the circle to dance with him alone, which is a significant sign of interest. The girls laughingly emit a rather suggestive "shu-shu-shu" sound as the dancing turns to a frenzy of twisting, wild motions while they shake their skirts in a provocative way at the young men. If a camera is present, as when a

This wedding celebration in Pacchanta followed a prescribed form known to all participants with no church ceremony or priest present.

foreigner visits, the young couple sometimes asks for a photo together adding a new dimension to courtship. Whether they ever see the photo is not as important as the act of having the picture taken. Flirting is similar to any singles bar anywhere, but in Pacchanta it occurs as the music from a small local band of musicians or a battery-powered tape player blares down the valley. Dancing followed by sneaking off together goes on, often until dawn's first light.

Weddings

Marriage marks an important passage of life when the duality of male and female join to become a new economic unit, a family, and a commitment. The couple may have proven that this is a fruitful union by producing several children already, but after some time they choose to officially marry, whether in the church or in a community ceremony outside the realm of the church. Pacchanta community marriages sometimes are recorded as civil marriages in Ocongate and sometimes the community gives them legitimacy. The family hosts drinking and dancing while attendees pin money on the groom and bride in Pacchanta in front of Apu Ausangate. Marriage clothing is the finest and is covered with meaningful symbols, while the attendees wear their best-woven symbols of Pacchantan identity.

Weddings are a time when all can gain merit by showing off their newest handiwork from their looms. Occasionally an unusual wedding takes place, such as the marriage of weaver Timoteo CCarita to Benita in Pitumarka.

When Timoteo CCarita, the mayor of Pitumarka, got married on October 20, he opted for what he called "an Inca-style wedding." He refused to get married in a business suit and instead wove two fine ponchos, one to wear and one folded over his shoulder. His first wife died after giving birth to four children. When Timoteo and Benita decided to marry, they chose a church wedding. Timoteo had gained status in the community when he took the two-year cargo as mayor of the town. It is rare for a Quechua artisan to become mayor of Pitumarka, but so many lawyers and administrators ran for the office that the vote was divided and Timoteo won. He and Benita had lived together for some time, and had two children. When Timoteo became mayor, the Church stepped up the pressure on them to get officially married. Women in Pitumarka are normally the weavers, but Timoteo is famous as an unusually fine weaver and Benita is also a proficient weaver. When they announced that they would marry in an "Inca style," it was not a surprise to most of the community but some

Timoteo and Benita were married in the Pitumarka church by a Catholic priest while wearing their finest woven clothing they had made for the wedding.

officials asserted that it was not appropriate for a government official. Timoteo took eight months to weave each poncho, not counting the spinning time.

He wore his ponchos with pride as they entered the partially restored church at about 9:30 A.M. and waited for the Catholic priest. Guests arrived and the priest finally showed up. Three barefooted men in fine ponchos, chullos, bayeta pants, and brown hats entered in procession followed by three women in polleras, ajotas, fancy ruffled blouses, llicllas, and old silver-trimmed montera hats. Benita wore fancy llicllas that she had made for the occasion and an ancestral gold-thread-trimmed montera.

The Catholic ceremony, performed by Padre David from Sicuani, was entirely in Quechua. The three men and women each held a candle. The marriage vows and ring exchange were accompanied by the traditional giving of old coins to the man from the woman who gives them back to the woman who then gives them back to the man, symbolically bringing prosperity to the couple by their joining together. The priest baptized their children after the wedding with the parents still in place after reciting the marriage vows.

The event then changed location to the courtyard of a nearby home where the wedding party stood around a natural alpaca kaypina (carrying cloth) spread flat on the ground. Each member of the wedding party made a speech, and then entered the covered, decorated eating area in a counterclockwise line around the textile. After a hot drink of quinoa and unleavened bread, potatoes with ocopa, egg and cheese were eaten, followed by a bowl of hot caldo or soup and finally the traditional roasted guinea pig and potatoes. The six members of the wedding party then ritually exchanged coca. The men traded their chuspas, each receiving coca from the other's bag. The women carried coca in their unkuna cloths and exchanged with the other women first, and then with the men.

Two old women appeared with bundles wrapped in carrying cloths and the traditional *wawatusuchiy* began. In Pitumarka and neighboring areas, traditional marriages include dancing with a large doll tied to your back in a carrying cloth. The two blond, blue-eyed dolls were adorned with fancy bonnets. A man receives the cloth and a large doll and then he asks the bride to dance with him. The other doll goes to a woman who dances with the groom. The dance started in the courtyard but dancers would occasionally race into the streets, around the town's main plaza, blessed by onlookers on their way back to the wedding courtyard. In this manner, the entire community joins the bride and groom in laughter and celebration. As each round of dancing ended, the two old women rescued the dolls to give to two new dance partners for the bride and groom. The previous partners would then enter the covered area to put wedding gifts of money on a plate for the bride and groom. While the activity was enjoyed with much laughter, fertility for the newlyweds was the main intention.

The party continued into the afternoon and evening with gifts arriving throughout the day, as *ollas* of chicha and cases of beer were consumed. Bulging kaypinas were given as gifts and costales (natural alpaca sacks) filled with potatoes completed commitments of ayni, return gifts of the same kind that Timoteo had given to others previously. Sixty-seven costales of ayni payments were reciprocated in addition to money and other gifts. Men helped transport the costales to Timoteo and Benita's house while Benita's female relatives symbolically put the carrying cloth gifts on their backs to carry home for her. The wedding party continued throughout the next day and night until everyone dropped from exhaustion.

Such a wedding symbolically brings together an asymmetrical but balanced union of male and female duality. This union, called *yanantin* in Quechua, symbolically joins the ayllus of the male and female in reciprocal commitments formed by the joining of man and woman. Each piece of traditional cloth and all objects used symbolically further the traditional way of doing things.

Death
Death seems frequent and harsh in the Andes, but all share in this transition. Bodies are viewed, prepared, and buried by the people, not intermediaries. Death is a known part of life and mourning accompanied by wailing is an active way of grieving. One day, a local boy leading his horse to Upis from

Pacchanta was killed when his leg became tangled in a rope and his horse fell on top of him. Another day a young mother in the hot springs had a seizure and drowned early one morning. Mauro's baby in Mahuayani died, after being left alone for only a moment by the mother. Quechuas understand that the relationships they have with the living do not end with death. After death, they feed the dead and converse with them on ritual occasions. How the passage into death occurs and is handled are important to the departing soul's well-being.

Ancestor worship is a popular phrase that scholars use to describe the continued relationships the living have with the dead. "Ancestor worship is one of the fundamental institutions of Andean society, and . . . certain huacas were shrines or places of important deceased persons. The deceased actively influence the health and well-being of the living, and . . . they employ the dead as documents "to delineate the rights and responsibilities of the living by keeping the dead close at hand." (Moseley 1992:53) The living do not so much worship the dead as they continue their relationships with them as ever-present spirits.

A ritual washing of the clothing of the dead person was a rite in Inca culture that continues today. Friends and family members visit the graves of loved ones with plates of their favorite foods and chicha or beer in November on All Souls Day. They talk with the dead, cry, laugh, and reminisce about the dead. The Inca people performed rites in November and December every year for the dead and gifts of cloth were offered to the souls of the dead. A mix of old and new occurred in Pacchanta one day when the grieving families were confronted by medics from Ocongate who performed an autopsy on the young girl who drowned because Peruvian national law demands an autopsy. Manuela, Maria's mother, wept and prayed all day for the soul of the girl, after she witnessed the medics slit the young woman's body right up the center. She felt that the cutting open of the body was dangerous for the girl's soul journey.

Natural Healing Rites and Offerings to the Gods

Healing rituals are rites aimed at rebalancing energies within bodies or communities that have become unbalanced or diseased. Misayoqs of the *paco* or pampamisayoq level can perform healing rituals. Well-known healers reside on the north coast, in the jungle, and in some highland areas. According to Quechua legends, while many Inca healers and religious leaders died with the Spanish conquest, others went into hiding in the *underground world,* one of the three realms of Inca cosmology including *hanan pacha* (upper world), *kaypacha* (this world), and *hurin pacha* (lower world). Some legends say these healer-shamans hid in the high mountains while others descended deep into the jungle regions where no one could find or bother them. They were able to continue the teachings and practices of their lineages based on the knowledge and wisdom of their ancestors. Many people today believe and know that these healers still exist and use natural healing and rituals.

In fact, natural healers do live in the jungles and highlands of Peru and are widely respected by local people for their abilities to heal with certain plants. Some prepare visionary plants such as *ayahuasca* and San Pedro. Scientists seeking cures for malaria found it in the natural medicine of the quinine tree in the Amazon jungle. Many modern pharmaceuticals derive from jungle environments. The interface of modern medicine and natural remedies is reaching a critical phase as the world's rainforest environments are destroyed to harvest lumber and to provide pasture for cattle. Trading natural resources, including indigenous peoples and animals' habitats and the natural medicines of the jungle, for short-term profit is a disaster of global proportions. Stories about healers are common. In the course of studying textiles used in ritual contexts, I encountered some remarkable men in the jungle and highlands, whose stories are worth recounting here.

Don Alejandro Jahuanchi, a Wachipayri Shaman

Over a ten-year period, Peter Frost, a Cuzco writer-journalist, my husband Ken, and I made the acquaintance of Don Alejandro Jahuanchi, a Wachipayri shaman. He was known as a lowland altomisayoq who lived in the jungle outside Pilcopata to the east of Paucartambo. A long dirt road that is covered by mud and lush green overgrowth in the rainy season links Pilcopata to the outside world, descending thousands of feet from the highlands near Tres Cruces. The alternate route, an even longer and more difficult overland journey, is sometimes taken from Ausangate via Markapata or Hatun Q'ero.

Don Alejandro believed medicines and cures for all diseases exist in the jungle environment. He called the jungle "the great pharmacy of *naturaleza.*" He said, "The plants, animals, and natural forces are the teachers and masters." He listened to the many voices and signs of naturaleza daily in the trees above his hut. "Kill only what you need, one animal, one tree. Remember, you take in not only what you eat but the diseases they have, the things they eat. . . . When the trees are cut, there is a great sadness in the jungle."

Alejandro, like other *curanderos* (healers), brought plants from the distant forest closer to his hut and cultivated a medicinal garden of specific plants that he kept ready to heal specific illnesses of the people who sought his help, while also continuing to search the jungle for certain wild plants he needed for healing. His knowledge of plants and healing had been passed from one healer to another through initiation.

"[Y]ou have to call the plant," he said. The plant is called a number of times in ceremony and each time it gets more meaningful and the relationship builds. The plant he referred to as the master vine of death and visions is ayahuasca. He believed healing with ayahuasca is accomplished by the combination of the plant and the shaman who can "call the plants" for healing. A number of medicinal plants are poisonous if not prepared correctly, so the healing rituals must be performed by a trained shaman. He said, "You must call the spirits, look for the colors, pray and listen. You must have will power, patience and faith, and above all, unconditional love. You must look in a mirror, see the past behind you and face the past, then you will be renewed in the colors."

In Don Alejandro's world, foods are taken directly from the jungle, especially the root of the *yuca,* a tuber of the jungle. About food he said, "The ancients were very clean, they knew what they were eating." He planted other foods certain animals like to eat near his hut to bring them closer to him. Human senses were tuned into the sounds of the jungle, with howler monkeys in the canopy treetops late in the afternoon, thousands of bees buzzing at once, and a slithering sound in the tall grass. No one was allowed to kill flies, insects, or bees when staying at Alejandro's hut simply because they cause humans some discomfort. "They have a right to live also," he said. He had no doors; thus creatures that slithered inside and curled up to sleep stayed there. He used gourd bowls, stating that plastic does not belong in the jungle. "You must be still," he said, to be engulfed in this world. "It takes one to other dimensions," he added.

[102, 103.] Altomisayoq Mariano Turpo (left) and Padre Antonio, the Catholic priest of Ocongate (right).

Don Alejandro was also a schoolteacher in Pilcopata, and loved by young children until his untimely death in 1998. New legends will now be told of a kind but firm contemporary shaman who lived in the eastern jungle and practiced with a knowledge of ancient healing in an area where mythology tells us the Inca shamans hid their wisdom of the natural world.

The Unlikely Friendship of Padre Antonio of Ocongate and Mariano Turpo of Alkaqocha

It is generally believed that people worship the mountains and earth. I believe they worship the spirits of the mountains and the earth. Through an altomisayoq, the most important religious specialist, one can achieve direct access to Roal, the creator spirit. People consult him, and receive instructions for solving their problems, and sometimes reprimands for improper attitudes or behavior. [Núñez del Prado 1974:243–45]

While living in Pacchanta and learning to weave with Maria's family and about Quechua culture, Maria's daughter Silea offered to accompany me one day on a three-hour walk up the mountain to

Alkaqocha to take gifts to her grandfather Mariano Turpo. Turpo was the altomisayoq living near Campa Pass who had originally read the coca leaves for me, prepared a despacho, and instructed me to stay with Maria. As we walked together talking, Silea pointed to large herds of alpacas, llamas, and sheep, and instructed me as to who owned them, where they lived in the valley, whose lands we were crossing, and where the most ferocious guard dogs for the herds and homes were. She was related to most of the families. We followed the ancestral water canal maintained by the widespread community of Pacchanta that runs down the north side of the valley bringing lake water to irrigate fields too high for river waters. We climbed up the trail about 1,500 feet to Mariano's house beside Alkaqocha Lake, which means the joining of two opposite but complementary relations, white and black in the realm of natural colors and light and dark in cosmological schemes. (Harrison 1989:51) Upon arrival, we encountered an extraordinary relationship between two men that caught me by surprise and taught us both much about unexpected places where Catholicism and indigenous beliefs overlap.

Mariano Turpo is referred to with the Spanish title of "don" and also as Wiraqocha, a term in Quechua for a gentleman or honored man. When I first met Mariano, Luis Pacsi had instructed me to address him as Wiraqocha due to his high status as a respected elder and ritual specialist. When I asked Mariano what he calls himself, he said *"hampeq,"* or one who knows, literally a curer or healer with medicines. Many people believe he is an altomisayoq who can call up any of the Apus or spirits, can cure with herbs and medicines, and can communicate directly as a mediator with the most powerful natural forces. Other people say all the altomisayoqs died out about twenty years ago, that no one of this status still lives today. An altomisayoq is the highest form of Andean ritual specialist. Pampamisayoqs are the next level, and these certainly still exist. They know how to celebrate specific rituals and conduct particular ceremonies for offerings to the Pachamama. They can cure the body and provide deep insight into various problems. (Flores Ochoa and Fries 1989:54) Yet another level is the kuraq akulleq (Yabar, cited in Bennett 1994:47; Núñez del Prado and Murillo 1996:117) Personally, I believe that Mariano is an altomisayoq who practices the ancient patterns he learned over half a century ago in his training. He lives alone at 16,000 feet, sends offerings to Apu Ausangate, and is visited by pampamisayoqs from the Q'ero region who treat him respectfully as an altomisayoq and a learned one. The events of the day that followed reinforced my belief.

When Silea and I arrived at Mariano's corral we asked permission from Mariano to enter the enclosure. We noticed two men sitting near him, one of whom was his son who now lives in Ocongate. The other was a Caucasian man probably in his late fifties, dressed in full indigenous traditional regalia—poncho, long white bayeta pants, an intricately knitted chullo, ajota sandals, and a brown felt hat adorned in the same way that Mariano had ceremoniously decorated his own hat. This odd man spoke fluent Quechua, preferring it to Spanish. The three who sat side by side were obviously performing some ritual together.

We presented the gift of coca I brought to thank Mariano for sending me to live with Maria in Pacchanta. The Caucasian man questioned me persistently in Quechua about my reason for being there. All three graciously accepted the coca and offered me some in exchange. This was my third trip to see Mariano. The first two times he had made despachos for me so I was comfortable with him and had come with his granddaughter to pay my respects and thank him.

I then asked the Caucasian where he lived, insinuating the same question, "What are you doing here?" He replied, "I live in Ausangate." I said, *"Kaypi?* Here?" He waved his arm toward the peaks and said, "Yes, all of here" in Quechua. His gesture was one of belonging and affection for the place. I said, "You mean up near the peaks?" Finally, smiling at me, he told me his name. He was Padre Antonio of the church in Ocongate, the main Catholic priest for the region, where he has lived for fifteen years. I recalled when Juan Núñez del Prado told me of a most unusual priest in Ocongate who liked to spend time out in the high places and how the indigenous people cared for him. I responded, "I have heard your name before, that you are greatly respected here." With a laugh he said in Spanish, "Someone has been telling you lies." I said, "No really, that is what they have told me." He was quiet for a few minutes and then said, "Yes, you are right. Some people say I am a good priest for the people and others say I am not a good priest at all."

They asked me questions about weaving, looking closely at my chuspa, the coca bag I had woven for myself, and then they went back to their ritual. They were tying t'ikas, literally flowers in Quechua, but here referring to yarn tassels to adorn the foreheads and tails of the horses. They prayed to the Apus together. Mariano looked up at me seriously and asked me if I wanted to take some pictures. I answered, "Yes, I would like to take photos." Everyone became much friendlier. I happened to notice the exceptionally intricate qocha pattern on Mariano's chullo. His son asked me if I liked coca and I said yes. They each offered me coca as a k'intu of leaves and we sat chewing coca together. Mariano's daughter-in-law brought Silea and me some chicha to drink from an undecorated, wooden kero cup of the same form as Inca keros.

Dusk was arriving, so Silea and I quickly started down the mountain back to Pacchanta catching a last sight of the three men huddled together sheltered near the house. Antonio intended to stay the night and the following day with Mariano. They continued together, this Catholic priest and the hampeq blessing the animals in joint ritual up near 16,000 feet on July 25, the day called Santiago by Catholics and the birthday of the animals according to indigenous beliefs.

I was perplexed as we descended past Alkaqocha (the black/white dual lake), Yanaqocha (black lake), Ñawi Qocha ("eye" lake), and Comerqocha (green lake) into the darkness. Suddenly, it occurred to me how many lakes are in this region, and as Silea named each one, I understood that the weavers were metaphorically creating their world in the textiles. In this world where I was a stranger, I sensed why weavers had such a rich vocabulary, annotating the variations in these lakes. The lakes were alive in the twilight. Was it the light or the ritual meeting I had just witnessed? Something changed my perception and allowed me to see.

Young girls participating in festival of the
Virgin of Carmen in Paucartambo, Peru.

Clothing, Masks, and Costumes as Signs of Identity

Rituals transform the order of the perceived world as well as distort conceptions of time and space. The senses experience an extraordinary assault of reversals, inversions, oppositions, and distortions that convert the logical world into intentional chaos. We then attempt to make sense of changes in sound, color, and the actions of masked characters.

During ritual activities with the adding of layers of cloth to form costumes and mask identity, perception is altered to that of another world or *otro mundo*. Solidarity of intent is expressed by wearing the same clothing as other human beings, such as a military uniform with assorted medals, or a nurse's white dress, but in festival wearing certain clothing marks not only identity but also at times a secret knowledge. Dancers know how to act in accordance with the character depicted by the clothing. They move as a unit, and each has his or her role.

Three ukuku dancers at Qoyllur Rit'i
pilgrimage, Ausangate.

Memories are associated with clothing and costumes. Perhaps an uncle or grandfather danced the same dance. Perhaps one's father wore the white tunic like Alejandro in the capacity of altomisayoq-shaman in the ayahuasca ceremony.

Like other peoples around the world, through clothing Quechuas express unity with their past, identify themselves with an ethnic or local group, and even manipulate it for greatest advantage in situations of conflict. Clothing, costumes, and adornment send powerful messages about the wearer, who they are, where they are from, and what concepts they agree or disagree with in life. This ability to communicate through clothing and costume is a learned behavior, and is equally relevant for a New York businessman in an expensive, black wool overcoat and Italian shoes; a gang member in all-black garb adorned with chains; a Balinese dancer with long tapered fingernails; a Tibetan monk in burgundy, gold, and orange robes; an Egyptian belly dancer in shiny, beaded gauze; and a shaggy costumed Quechua ukuku dancer. People possess knowledge of what constitutes belonging in certain groups, which is expressed in the rules of appropriate attire for personal gain or membership.

Sometimes these rules are displayed unconsciously, and at other times they are deliberately manipulated. I have witnessed indigenous men from Ausangate in truck beds headed for Cuzco remove their ponchos and replace them with a manufactured zippered pullover emblazoned with the word "Adidas," and take off their chullos, leaving only the secondary felted hat on their heads. In doing so, they remove their community identity into a more generic statement of "peasant" for their interactions in the city. Based on experience, they know they will suffer less discrimination if they appear to be less "Indian." These same men climb back into the trucks for the return trip to their communities and upon nearing their homelands, they throw on their ponchos, place the chullo under their felt hat, and proudly repossess their rural respected identity. This clothing exchange process helped me gain a better understanding of why many city dwellers assert that all indigenous people are losing their traditions, changing their clothing, and no longer weaving fine textiles.

Manipulation of identity takes place in everyday life and in festival costumes. Coded messages are expressed in how a costume is put together. Revisiting the ukuku character and the bear-like (and possibly llama-alpaca) costume is worthwhile for deeper insight into his true nature and identity.

This kindred spirit to the clown/trickster in North America crosses worlds and realigns energies. In North American Pueblo rituals, the clown acts out what has most troubled the religious leaders and the society throughout the past year. These concerns are translated into native terms by the clown's actions, humor, and satire. The trickster reinforces mythical tradition but is capable of change. The clown or trickster re-presents the world. (Alfonso Ortiz, conversation with author, Albuquerque, New Mexico, 1993) "The dual role played by Pueblo clowns and also by Plains Indians is of contraries, who always did things backward. The clowns' responsibility is to cheer people up when they are downcast, but also to bring people back-to-earth when they begin to think too highly of themselves." (Fools Crow, cited in Mails 1991:115)

The ukuku, wearing the shaggy, black, hairy suit, carrying a doll in his own image and speaking in a high falsetto voice, is the humorist, the jokester. But he also plays the role of the stern disciplinarian, the one who brings laughter but maintains order while adding to the chaos. Let's assume that this character is a bear. The only bear in Peru other than the costumed ukuku is the Andean spectacled bear, living mostly in the high jungle between the mountains and the low jungle. They exist in small numbers, forage only at dawn and dusk, and are known to feed on cultivated crops. "The bear passes between the highlands and the lowlands, day and night . . . [I]t lives in caves and connects this world to the underworld and the spirit world." (Randall 1982:56)

Allen (1983:43) says the bear is a combination of awkwardness and power, and is a symbol of the indigenous people who in national society are seen as wild, illiterate, inexperienced, and uncivilized. The puma and the condor as

These *diablo* or devil dancers hanging on a balcony intimidating onlookers at the festival of Paucartambo are a good example of distortion, reversal, and unusual social roles during festival.

symbols of the Inca empire were transformed into the bear as a symbol of indigenous cleverness seen under a guise of clumsy awkwardness. The bear thus becomes an outspoken metaphor for the indigenous way of dealing with conquest and an unspoken symbol among Quechua people.

Another indigenous character is the chuncho who wears a headdress with macaw tail feathers waving high in the air in a brilliant display of color. Chuncho dancers perform in many festivals including Qoyllur Rit'i, and the motif is still woven into textiles in Q'ero. The chuncho character represents the savage from the past, the *ñawpa*. He is a tribal inhabitant of the lowland jungle who is in opposition to the Qolla highlander or the civilized world. Chunchos often symbolically battle with mankind during festivals and are sent back to the past or to the jungle from where they came.

These characters act out the nature of indigenous creatures, expressing not only a collective understanding of myth but also memory of the past that does not appear in textbooks. The mask has its own power. In recent years, the number of dance groups at Pentecost in Ollantaytambo has increased because more young people wish to dance, and because of the village's income from tourism, they can afford the costumes. All of these groups have strict rules for membership, and exact requirements of costume, movement, and behavior. In the enactment of metaphor, reality is malleable and becomes contended terrain, and participants are allowed to vent hostilities under the cover of festival space-time.

Reversals, Inversions, Distortions, and Renewed World Order

The concept of world order reversal and rebirth is symbolically conveyed when the world wakes up the morning after chaotic days and nights during Qoyllur Rit'i to a sense of calm and renewed order. Qoyllur Rit'i is said to connect that chaotic period in the Inca calendar represented by the disappearance of the Pleiades with the symbolic time of transition from a past world order into a new one. (Randall 1982) At the Paucartambo festival, the Virgin of Carmen solemnly begins the festival on Friday night with Sunday afternoon being overtaken by chaos as yellow paint and beer are sprayed at the crowd and devils prance openly on balconies above the plaza. Distortion adds to chaos through enlarged features and body parts and exaggerated masks, such as the *diablo* masks. In festival time, humankind enters a state of chaos and with the help of the gods regains order.

A precedent for the idea of ritual reversal existed in the Inca worldview known as a *pachacuti,* literally "when what is up goes under and what is under comes up." (MacCormick 1991) It is a time of transition from one age to another. "In the middle and most dramatically at the end of each age a period of upheaval known as a pachacuti (world reversal) takes place. Uprightness is symbolic of order and morality. Being hung upside down was a common Inca punishment for crimes. Upside down symbolized disorder and immorality but was considered a cyclical cleansing and return." (Classen 1993a:122)

The Inca concept of duality of *hanan* and *hurin* expressed the upper/lower, light/dark, left/right, male/female, sun/moon, wet/dry, lowlands/highlands, and allowed for power to move from the underworld to the upper world and return again. "Duality is better defined by the term *a dual organization* because it is not static, but dynamic and complementary in the existence of the two oppositional forces. A more fundamental problem is that of understanding just how a society can be divided and united at the same time, and how it continues through time." (Ortiz 1969:8–9) Time and space are distorted, and for the Andean mind there can be no division between time and space. The Quechua word "*pacha*," meaning time and space and earth in one word, underscores this unity. (Randall 1982)

"In the destruction of things, it is a way to get from one order to another." (Alfonso Ortiz, conversation with author, Albuquerque, New Mexico, 1993) Ritual release defuses problems before they explode, with even more blood being shed. Bloodshed during ritual is perceived in some situations to release built-up tensions in the society. Rituals allow expressions of faith as well as resistance, but they also provide disorder, chaos, and upheaval to reign briefly. Then through ritual and offerings, humankind can regain a sense of order and a revised balance in the world. The process is one of renewal.

In the end, these legends are not merely told for enjoyment or for education or for amusement: they are believed. They are emblems of a living religion, giving concrete form to a set of beliefs and traditions that link people living today to ancestors from centuries and millennia past. As Bronislaw Malinowski said, myth in its living, primitive form is not merely a story told but a reality lived. [Erdoes and Ortiz 1984:xv]

CHAPTER NINE

Transitions within Cultures and the Mask of Progress

What [indigenous] peoples are struggling for now,

as indeed in the earlier periods, is not the hope

of remaining in pristine otherness. That is a Western

fantasy that gets projected on[to] indigenous people

all the time. Rather[,] people are very clear that they

are struggling for self-determination, that is[,] significant

control over the terms and conditions under which

they will develop their relations with the nation-state,

the global economy, the communication revolution,

expansionist Christianity, and other historical processes.

—Pratt (1999:39)

Tradition is dynamic and capable of change without becoming extinct. However, consideration of traditional forms of cultural continuity, such as rituals and weavings, cannot ignore the impact of contemporary outside influences on the Quechua worldview. Such influences should not be misconstrued as cultural contamination, which implies blind acceptance by the indigenous world in the manner of a disease spreading out of control. Influences are introduced factors working on indigenous choices that when made by individuals or groups are incorporated into individual lives and textiles without necessarily changing the basic core of the Andean worldview. While natural processes of birth, growth, maturity, and death continue inexorably, innovation is allowed within hereditary structures balanced with long-established rules of appropriateness in expression of identity through dress, art, and ritual. The Pachamama—Mother Earth to Quechuas—endures as the perpetual center of all existence as when her grasses sprout, strengthen, are eaten or die of old age as do all her varied forms of life. According to the Quechua worldview, all these many varied life forms are connected, and all are forms of energy. Spring does not exist without winter. Spirit resides in every person, animal, and object, and this natural creative force survives or declines in relationship to all things.

It is not uncommon then to acknowledge and expect change. While Western culture cherishes permanence in material things, Quechuas seek efficiency or utility but certainly not without aesthetics. A highly developed sense of aesthetics is used by indigenous weavers in decisions about making and using weavings based on the Inca concept of nonseparation of beauty, form, function, and the sacred in everyday life. Objects made for functional use as well as rituals are expected to go through transitional stages and eventually wear out. A weaving is created and highly prized when worn, but is not hidden or left unused in order to preserve it. Beauty and practicality may join to create an aesthetic desired for both everyday and sacred realms.

It is worthwhile, at certain hours of the day or night, to look closely at useful objects at rest. Wheels that have crossed long, dusty distances with their enormous loads of crops or ore, sacks from coal, barrels, baskets, the handles and hafts of carpenters' tools. The contact these objects have had with the earth serve as a text for all tormented poets. The worn surfaces of things, the wear that hands give to them, the air, sometimes tragic, sometimes pathetic, emanating from these objects lends an attractiveness to the reality of the world that should not be scorned. [Neruda 1985:30]

Indigenous people are faced with choices about material objects that may change their way of life. In Janchipacha, a woman spins while her son rests on his bike.

The changing utility of objects was illustrated to me in an experience that began when Maria gave me a baby sheep. The mother had refused to nurse it so we tried feeding it with a bottle of prepared dried milk. We called it my *wawa,* my baby. Since I was childless, the women often mentioned to me how I needed to have at least one child. But the symbolic baby died. I mourned the death and they buried it at my request. Later that same day, I found that the body had been dug up and discretely hidden on top of the pile of dung fuel on the lower side of the hearth inside the house. The softness of a baby sheep pelt was far too valuable to be buried unused. This is the material needed for the sacred type of coca bags made exclusively for misayoqs to carry their coca. They are visually recognized by their possession of this bag, as no one else should use them. In the changing of natural form, the pelt had an efficiency as well as aesthetic in death. Useless waste of natural resources does not make sense nor do attempts to deny changes experienced in the sensory world of nature.

While changes in the natural world are accepted, where do changes associated with the concepts called *progress and globalization* or the homog-enization of distinctive cultures fit into this worldview? Jorge Flores Ochoa, a well-known anthropologist at the Universidad Nacional de San Antonio de Abad in Cuzco, asked his audience one night while lecturing about the real meaning of progress to Latin America: "What do we gain and what is lost? Does progress mean the same from our perspective as [compared to that of] the Western world?"

Latin Americans represent an enormous workforce and resource supply for the modern (or perhaps post-modern) world. They also represent consumers to corporations. The expansion of the national infrastructure includes the con-struction of new roads into remote regions. Medicines, tools, and many other types of manufactured goods arrive in heavily loaded trucks from the cities. Merchants sell the manufactured goods while simultaneously introducing values of mass consumerism into local markets. Are people's lives enriched?

Quechua people are faced with choices about accepting or rejecting objects from the modern world based on their own indigenous habits and values. Cultural diversity works to preserve cultural differences. Indigenous people want a voice, which means the right to self-determination and thus the right to make their own choices. Quechua people refuse to forget their heritage, including their Inca mythology, because it is part of their identity. "A people can no more function without this sort of mythology than an individual can function without a nervous system. . . . It is the organizing principle of all our actions. It explains to us the meaning of everything we do." (Quinn 1996:277)

Progress is defined in a standard English-language dictionary as "to move forward, proceed, to develop to a more advance stage, improve." Dr. Flores Ochoa posed the questions of what do Peruvians gain from being a workforce for foreign and national investors, and from relegating the earth to the status of a raw materials source for industry rather than as a mother to indigenous peoples and the source of life. What does television with programming from Lima give to indigenous communities? I remembered our small family huddled around our first Zenith 14-inch, black-and-white television in 1955 as I noticed three teenaged Quechua girls staring through an open door at a television transmitting *Baywatch* in the truck stop restaurant in Ocongate, Peru. What do they think of these bikini-clad women running across sunny beaches? As they giggle nervously staring at these racing images, does it make them suddenly want to move to cities and wear such minimal clothing? Even with all these outside influences, in some remote areas highland girls are still more interested in retaining ancestral pride in being Quechua and learning new weaving pallay than going to live in the cities and wearing manufactured clothing made by someone they don't even know.

The nation-state of Peru is dedicated to the incorporation of the indigenous population into the national economy. New values are introduced with road building and installation of electrical power lines providing access to television. When international and national programmers portray indigenous people, the characterizations are usually simple, romanticized images marketed to attract profitable tourism. Indigenous life is not so simple; a harsh reality exists.

But on the other side, indigenous peoples' lives are rich in meaning, spirit, and symbology. The lengthy narratives of ritual and textile interactions in this text have attempted to show the texture and depth of meanings retained in the rituals and art forms of Quechua people. The wealth experienced directly here is not necessarily in quantities of material possessions but in local aesthetics and appreciation of a reality held together by a shared past and ongoing community. Outsiders are quick to label this world poor in material comforts and possessions. This concept is not Quechua any more than it is for a young native Alaskan man who called into National Public Radio recently and said, "We did not know we were poor until people came up here and called us poor." Native Americans, including Quechuas, became acquainted with the idea of being called poor when the idea of progress reached their communities. Forms of education have changed and in the context of national economic and political structures, education represents the key to the indigenous voice being heard. Quechuas, like many other indigenous peoples, are looking for new ways to deal with and participate in national politics and economy, including how to break the rules for their own benefit.

Oscar Arias, former president of Costa Rica and Nobel Peace Prize recipient, campaigns for change in Latin American governmental policies toward what progressive countries call the "underprivileged." He challenges nation-states to demonstrate compassion for the rights of indigenous peoples. He advocates an end to military spending and calls for an educated population as the best guarantee for a redefinition of democracy in Latin American nations. Arias describes education as the "single greatest weapon for development and expansion of consciousness in Latin America." (Arias 2000)

Such demands, coupled with the growing volume of indigenous leaders' voices throughout Latin America, call world attention to the inadequacies of current educational philosophy and policies in Ausangate and other indigenous communities. Historically, education was denied to Quechuas around

Ausangate. Hacienda Lauramarka encompassed 64,000 hectares, the entire north side of Ausangate "as far as one can see" (Luis Pacsi, conversations with author, Ausangate, Peru, 1996), including the district capital of Ocongate. On December 6, 1969, it was the first highland hacienda affected by the land reform bill promulgated by President Juan Velasco Alvarado in June 1969. "This particular hacienda occupies a distinguished place in Peruvian rural history as it exemplifies the tenacity, the courage and the determination of indigenous [people] who refused to be cowed by abuses, . . . exploitation

and even . . . murders perpetrated against them over the years." (Gow 1976:139) During the revolt of Túpac Amaru in 1780, the whole area supported him, particularly the town of Ocongate. (Valcárcel 1970:176, cited in Gow 1976:148) This area, which includes Pacchanta, has a rebellious past; indigenous people struggled for centuries to gain and regain grazing rights and freedom from servitude. They were continually legislated against in Lima on behalf of wealthy landowners and served as an example to other indigenous people. (Gow 1976:148) Freedom from servitude and the right

Children receiving a gift of pencils and notebooks at the local rural school in Pacchanta, with Ausangate in background.

to education came hard for this area. The altomisayoq Mariano Turpo, now ninety-two years old, was one of the primary advocates for freedom from servitude to hacienda owners.

Rural public schools attempted to take the place of Quechua community education. In the early twentieth century, the "Indian problem" was a major concern for the government in Lima. In the 1940s, government policies, based on the notion that indigenous values were a hindrance to progress, attempted to assimilate the indigenous population through propagation of the Spanish language. This study of textiles and rituals is not a political exposé, but it is difficult to discuss the heritage of the people of Ausangate or consider the perseverance of the Quechua worldview without considering the new role of public education on the lives of weavers and their children and communities. While education is critical, it is important to look deeper into the its content and who controls it.

In Peru, six years of public education is compulsory. However, local rural schools funded by the national government provide only the most basic level of education. First-year primary school is sometimes taught in Quechua (but not always), followed by all-Spanish instruction. Children come to school having learned Quechua as their first language at home. Teachers have been customarily trained in cities such as Cuzco or Sicuani. While the teachers may or may not be native Quechua speakers, part of the objective of public education policy is to integrate indigenous people into the national economy, which requires knowledge of Spanish. In Pacchanta, I observed the teaching of math, basic Spanish, health, and Peruvian history in the local rural primary school.

Many newly trained teachers are forced to spend their first two years of employment teaching in the countryside before they can get a good job in the cities. Most do not like their rural assignments. They travel back to the cities as often as they possibly can for meetings or to visit their families. In 1996, the typical teacher's salary in Pacchanta and surrounding communities was about $200 per month or about $6.50 per day. In Hatun Q'ero, the teacher's weekend jaunts often turned into five-day absences. Teachers did not have to account for their absences. In Pacchanta, classes were frequently cancelled for a week for meetings or some other purpose requiring the teacher to return to Cuzco for the week.

Students at the rural school in Hapu (Q'ero region), who luckily had books and an enthusiastic teacher. (2002)

At harvest time, children were needed by their families to help in the fields and did not attend classes. The reality of compulsory education is approximately three years and most children who achieve this level of education are boys. According to Oscar Núñez del Prado (1973:45), "There was greater resistance to the girls having to go to school, because their parents felt that learning to read or write would be of no use to them, since in the daily activities of the family it is the males who deal with problems and handle relations with outsiders." While this appears to be a gender bias statement, many parents did not believe that public education was beneficial for their children in its present form. Some believed that it was more important for girls to weave and help at home. Marcelino Moralez from Huaraz told me one day, "Many of the people in the highlands believe schools give our children ideas about leaving the community for the cities and we do not like that. Some go away to Lima and never come back."

On the other hand, for some of the highland population, schools represent better lives formerly denied them by the Catholic Church, local hacendados, and the Spanish colonial government. Until the breakdown of the hacienda system during the Velasco regime in the 1970s, educating

Indians was considered dangerous. "[C]hildren were obligated to attend classes daily, early in the morning, and were supposed to be taught prayers, the catechism, church music, reading and writing. The instruction in reading and writing was seldom given in practice. Spaniards had a deep mistrust of literate Indians." (Rowe 1957:188) "The Archbishop of Puno, on a pastoral visit to Chucuito, exploded with rage when he discovered two Indian schools staffed by Indian teachers. He informed the Indians that they should dedicate themselves to agriculture rather than education because otherwise they would fall in with Indians in league with the devil." (Gow 1976:109)

When indigenous people were given the right to vote by the Velasco regime, political workers headed to the highlands, where roads existed, and distributed pictures, painted names, symbols, and slogans on walls, hung posters, and proclaimed the virtues of political parties and politicians on loudspeakers. Public schools and electricity followed these roads, as did merchants. Reading, writing, schools, and politicians clamoring for indigenous votes brought the traditional highlanders into the modern world.

For the Peruvian national government, rural schools represent a resource for bringing the Quechua highlanders into the national economy and political system. During his campaign for reelection in 1995, former President Alberto Fujimori established high targets for continuing the construction of new rural schools. In 1996, when I spent a lot of time in Pacchanta and visited surrounding communities, the government's policy was to construct as many new rural schools as possible, but this policy did not include providing teachers, furniture, materials, books, and pens or pencils for students. It did, however, increase Peru's likelihood of receiving World Bank loans.

Uniforms in rural schools were more flexible than in urban schools. Boys sometimes carried what looked like a book bag, but was handwoven with traditional designs for carrying the small notebooks their families provided for them. Silea, Maria's daughter, was not allowed to spin yarn while sitting in class nor could she wear her montera hat. A Quechua woman removes her hat only to eat, enter a church, and sleep. The time she spent in school was time she could not spend with her mother, grandmother, and her aunts learning more complex weaving patterns and techniques and how to become a correct Quechua woman. School often gave young people ideas about leaving the community for the cities, such as working as maids in homes in Cuzco, but it did not reinforce community values like wearing the pallay did. Silea was a bright girl who attended school more than others. In 2000, Maria told me that Silea was living in Puno working as a vendor. But in 2001 when I returned,

Two young Quechua girls, Pitumarka Valley.

Silea was home in Pacchanta herding her animals and raising her son Jon William by herself. While it appears that she seized an opportunity for a better life through gaining an education, the pros and cons of leaving her community for city life and giving up weaving were certainly debatable issues.

The nation-state is proud of rural education mandated from Lima but the reality calls for Quechua teachers in the schools to teach respect for persistent indigenous values. The government of Peru is constructing rural schools as mentioned to teach Quechua children the Spanish language, and to try to integrate Quechua culture into the national political system and economy. This worldview suggests that indigenous people should give up their ancestral patterns of life because they are difficult and keep them impoverished, in order to participate in the national workforce. However, such participation in the past has contributed to someone else's financial gain rather than theirs. Rural education contains little instruction about pre-Conquest civilizations—except when useful for the promotion of tourism—because this does not contribute to the government's desire for a pacified peasantry.

The rural schools are a disaster. The teachers do not explain concepts in Quechua, for instance, to explain the shape of the world, the sun, the moon, and rotation. Words do not exist in Spanish or English to explain these ideas to a Quechua child. The laws for education come from Lima and they do not understand highland ways of thinking. [Gloria Tamayo, professional Quechua instructor and tutor, interview by author, Cuzco, Peru, 10 August 1996]

Peru is not alone among Latin American nations in its struggle to provide education for the indigenous population and in its desire to increase national productivity. Nor are Quechuas as indigenous people alone in attempting to uphold their way of life. Foreigners are taking more interest in helping the indigenous voice to be heard worldwide as in the case of the Kogi, the contemporary descendants of the Tairona who live isolated from the modern world by an impenetrable jungle barrier. When British author and documentary filmmaker Alan Ereira arrived in the 1980s, the Kogi permitted him to film them and record their practices, worldview, and message, and then he was told to get out and never come back. Their message taped by the BBC, as the isolated Elder Brother to the modern Younger Brother was, "*[Y]ou are taking the heart out of the mother, the earth. You must stop this before it is too late.*" (Ereira et al. 1991) While the Kogi retreated centuries ago to their high ground and have lived relatively untouched by the modern world, today other educated indigenous leaders are expressing similar worldviews and viewpoints, thereby supplying vital insights into their own future and ours as well. Indigenous education must be reformed to embrace their own version of history and to disseminate their perspectives about humankind's relationships to the natural environment—for the sake of all of us.

Today our concerns are of a new order. Can what was originally communicated through the oral tradition be converted to the printed word, without losing the nuances and vitality of the spoken word, in light of the gradual passing of the older generation? Can succeeding generations continue the oral tradition in spite of having been greatly affected by the printed word and electronic media? What will be the impact of the fact that educated natives must read about their own traditions from the academic perspectives of anthropology, sociology, literature and religion? [Amiotte 1992:34]

Alternative Forms of Education: Revitalization Programs

Indigenous education takes new forms other than that of the state university or rural primary schools, occasionally accomplishing a marriage of old and new. Education can be based more on the experiential rather than knowledge largely dependent on reading. Revitalization programs based on disseminating information at the local level though community organizations, such as mothers' clubs or weaving groups, are gaining momentum. These programs are frequently initiated by government officials or outside interests but they come to be controlled by indigenous leaders who educate their participants not only in revitalizing forgotten weaving techniques, new products for a foreign market and business strategies, but also instill pride rather than shame in being indigenous. These programs are markedly different from others because leaders are local indigenous people and women often voice opinions and strategies.

Some Andean communities initiating revitalization programs are attempting to prevent their young people from moving to cities in search of work and in the process forgetting their heritage. Such indigenous groups are interested in educating foreign visitors about the complicated techniques of backstrap weaving and the value of handmade cloth in a highly commercialized modern world. These programs help create external markets for traditional textile arts and enable weavers to better control the forms of their own creativity.

In 1996, Nilda Callañaupa, a Quechua weaver from Chinchero, Peru, along with supportive friends, founded the Center for Traditional Textiles of Cuzco. As a child, Nilda learned to spin on a drop spindle and to weave cosmological symbols from her Quechua grandmothers in Chinchero. She said, "Here in Peru weaving is an art that we lived every day and for us it is more than an art—it is a historical part of the living culture. We are fortunate that many of our practices are still alive and can be continued. But they are changing fast and are in danger of being lost." Nilda has helped organize a group of Chinchero weavers who continue to weave traditional styles and teach older techniques to the community. They work with international tour groups to demonstrate the old natural dyes and weaving techniques to draw local communities' attention to the pride they can take in their textile heritage.

Nilda Callañaupa, a Quechua weaver from Chinchero, crosses international boundaries to sustain traditional weaving in Cuzco. With the help of friends, she founded the Center for Traditional Textiles of Cuzco.

In Pitumarka, Peru, Timoteo CCarita uses plant and mineral natural

ABOVE, LEFT: These Chinchero weavers provide textile education for foreigners by demonstrating their technical processes with detailed explanation in English to help maintain their textile heritage and way of life.

ABOVE, RIGHT: Chinchero weaver working on a belt loom.

dyes to dye sheep and alpaca wool for the colonial style of weaving that he is personally renewing. While serving as the mayor of his community, he initiated a program through the local mothers' club to teach women to weave on backstrap looms again, a process some had forgotten.

Weavers have learned a complicated, four-section, supplemental, warp-scaffolding technique used in Inca times from one of the oldest women weavers in the community who still remembered the technique. The significance of the number four during the Inca empire era is evidenced from the Inca name for the empire itself, Tahuantinsuyo, which meant the four parts joined together in a unified whole.

While the meaning of the four sections in the weaving is not exactly the same today, weavers still take pride in weaving the complicated structures of the past. This group of over fifty weavers has evolved technically, and is now creating textiles of sixteen intricate parts, thereby pushing themselves beyond what their ancestors achieved. Young men and women realize that they can now make a living at weaving, thus renewing their interest and pride in this endeavor.

My role as facilitator and weaver has been reciprocal with all of these programs. I have served as a guide for groups from the Maxwell Museum of Anthropology and the Yale Alumni Association, among others, who have engaged the weavers, gained a better understanding of their goals, and provided an economic stimulus to their high-quality production projects. While one might argue that we are agents of change, higher prices are paid directly to the producers in underdeveloped areas. This is readily noticeable when the Quechua weavers from the surrounding villages meet me and the foreign groups with great enthusiasm many miles above their village. My

In Pitumarka, Daphne Ccarita works on a scaffold warp weaving as part of the Mother's Club revitalization program.

The warp-scaffolding technique revived by Pitumarka group members through the use of discontinuous warp allows them to make a four-section weaving. As of 2001, they had produced sixteen-part weavings.

The revitalization group includes weavers from Pitumarka, and from as far away as Tinta, shown here working with Timoteo CCarita.

role is that of a cultural and economic broker supporting such revitalization programs in Peru and Bolivia.

The Antropólogos del Sur Andino (ASUR) program in Sucre, Bolivia, under the directorship of Veronica Cereceda, houses a museum of the villages of Tarabuco's and Jalq'a's (also known as Potolo) past with contemporary textile arts for sale in the museum gift shop. Foreign visitors are educated by the ongoing exhibits in the museum, view indigenous weavers at work, and then can make informed purchases of high-quality wall hangings made for the outside market at the source. A new program aided by the mayor of Potosí has helped more than two hundred Calcha weavers market directly to tourists visiting one of the finer restaurants of the city. They are innovating with useful new shapes for tourists but not compromising their own aesthetic values and reputations for tightly woven textiles.

The ASUR program is an excellent example of the use of museum exhibitions with an indigenous voice to communicate directly to tourists about local aesthetics for high-quality textiles, which enables weavers to keep producing high-quality weavings for external markets. Museums can help play a vital role in the future through the inclusion of indigenous voices as curators, in-house exhibit directors, and consultants for artistic and ethnographic exhibits about indigenous cultures. Some innovative museums are already responding to the challenge of rethinking their roles in the twenty-first century.

> I confess that I find the entire notion of revitalization a trifle culturally hidebound, for I suspect that if we had a comparably rich texture of historical detail for other cultures as we have for the Pueblos we would find that revitalization is not a challenge come uniquely to them under the impact of industrial civilization, but, truly, a regularly reoccurring imperative. What we are dealing with here, I believe, are several distinctive manifestations of a universal and noble human aspiration—namely, the will to endure. [Ortiz 1994:305]

Tourism and Cultural Preservation

Not all meetings of tourism and local arts are resolved via the educational intent that revitalization programs are seeking. Tourism, like conquest, brings two cultures together in the same geographic location. According to some schools of thought, tourism is different from military or political conquest because it casts one culture as host to the other cultural group. The hosts often

Textile shoppers during the annual festival of Santiago Isla Taquile, Lake Titicaca.

provide needed basic services such as meals, accommodations, infrastructure for travel, and local guides to tell the visitors of the significance of sites, legendary heroes, mythology, and other local lore. Logically, the rules for guests' behavior would seemingly be established by the host culture. However, given that tourism is a consumer activity, often the visitors' rules become norms for aesthetics and for interaction. The host culture seeks the influx of tourist dollars to boost the local economy. The foreign visitor or tourist seeks to better understand the culture they are experiencing and to purchase local arts. Local art production or crafts made exclusively for sale to foreigners are adapted to market demands based on introduced aesthetics. Some ritual events are even adapted to accommodate the shorter nonindigenous attention span due to limited understanding of the deeper context of the ritual, as well as the particular group and individual's schedule. However, educated local guides acting as cultural interpreters can help bridge the crevasse of understanding when two cultural worldviews engage.

What is gained and what is compromised through tourism? Certainly producers of what Nelson Graburn (1976) called "tourist and ethnic arts" gain income. Consumers gain diversion from their work lives, restful retreats, and material reminders of a world apart from the complex world that they inhabit. Tourists are attracted by a sense of adventure or appreciation for the exotic that is not available in their post-modern work or home environments, and they experience a brief sense of connectedness to another world.

The artisans who carve wood, weave or sew miniature cloth garments

A Pacchantan knitter makes miniature chullos quickly and with ease to sell to trekkers and foreigners as a remembrance of Ausangate.

make a living, and sometimes create their own original forms in smaller versions. When indigenous people produce objects for consumer demand—and I am not referring to hourly wage earning jobs but rather to those artistic styles related to what they make for themselves—the relevant question is, "[D]o they continue to produce objects based on ancestral and local aesthetics for themselves?" (Graburn 1976:32) Does tourist demand for clothing, artifacts, souvenirs, postcards, photos, and memory-stirring objects dictate what indigenous produce for the market? Indigenous artists, like any artists, are faced with ethical and artistic considerations of why they are artists. Art is a process of expression of worldview and in this case, it collides with the aesthetic systems of outsiders' cultural values. For these reasons, revitalization programs put the ball back in the indigenous ballpark.

Globalization and Cultural Identity

In the context of economic "globalization," are we really all striving to look alike? We are definitely not. Consumers spend billions of dollars trying to carve out their identities based on available resources, but most people no longer have the time nor do they wish to make their own garments. We archive information in our minds from the visual presence of others based on how they assemble the parts of their presentation in their daily lives or in ritual. We sense others' identities from their odor, the multifaceted look they adopt, the textures they combine, and what we see them eat and how they enjoy it. Whether we choose polleras and flat, fringed hats, pierce our bodies in hundreds of previously unheard of places, or tattoo large expanses of skin, we express who we are, what we think, and how we identify ourselves. Our actions within this visual array of conglomerated parts further express the message of who we are and what groups we belong to. What we choose to take off and expose also communicates particular messages. Through active choices, Quechuas, like everyone else, express their identity. While some choose to adopt manufactured dress, others continue to construct their own cloth and costumes with a sense of communal pride, not just out of habit but also to communicate belonging.

Wearing particular garments during rituals continues to establish solidarity among participants in the face of modernization, post-modernization, and globalization. Through the ongoing fashioning of visual metaphors in textiles and the enactment of mythological knowledge during festivals and rituals, some Quechua people continue to express their own unique identity in a way of life that has survived centuries of change. At this very moment somewhere in the Andes, young girls are learning ancestral codes of knowledge while young men are sewing sequins on their costumes for next year's festival, as Quechua culture renews itself through its textiles and rituals in the way of the old ones because "this is he way things have always been done."

An old myth tells the story of Inkarri, who, representing the Inca, lost his head and went into hiding in the underworld at the time when the Spanish Conquest interrupted the last pachacuti. In the future, Inkarri will be reunited with his head, weavers will weave his image with his head proudly reconnected. These developments will bring in the next transition or new world order. In Quechua beliefs, the past is in front of our bodies while the future is behind us. Imagine that as Quechuas and the rest of us look back over our shoulders at the future, we see a glimpse of Inkarri, the new indigenous leader made of past and present, with his body and head reattached, dressed in his distinctive unku and traditional clothing, proudly leading his people based on respect for the Pachamama. Or was that a headless man just hit by a huge Volvo truck roaring down a rural dirt road headed for market loaded with vendors and young foreign tourists sitting on top of freshly cut lumber from the jungle? Will this mythological vision of a transformed world order occur before the current one destroys the Pachamama? This story has no ending. It continues to unmask itself as an ongoing process of ceaseless change, innovation, insistent resistance, and powerful spirits.

Julia Flores, Mamacha T'ika (Mother Flower)

Yesterday in front of your weaving shop
Across from the town's dilapidated Catholic church,
We drank homebrewed *chicha,* local corn beer together.
Nearby, quietly the massive Inca granite stone
Still looks like a sacred table for ancient gods.
This morning you walk to the train station to sell
Brilliant tapestries held high in front of your face.
While foreigners on the Machu Picchu train haggle prices,
My godchild, your newborn, is wrapped
In a hand-woven cloth securely tied to your back.
You sell a tourist a textile for twenty-four dollars
In the ten minute pause the train makes in the station.
Foreigners, heavy with money, buy through the windows.
Then the train passes as fast as the smoke clears and
You walk back to your store passing by the quiet stone.
Laughing, you cradle my shoulders, as we sit together
Like the *Quechua mamacha,* Inca ruins above us.
The sun will rise tomorrow as you return to the station.
There, they will see only an Indian market woman,
A pobre, Julia, you with such wealth around and within you.

—By Andrea M. Heckman REPRINTED WITH PERMISSION OF THE
AMERICAN ANTHROPOLOGY ASSOCIATION, FROM THE
Journal of Humanistic Anthropology 26, NO. 1 (JUNE 2001)

FACING PAGE: This contemporary Pacchantan woman continues wearing
her indigenous clothing with a colorful lake-patterned lliclla across
her back identifying to all who understand that she is from Ausangate.

GLOSSARY

acllawasi	women of the Inca empire specially chosen to weave the finest textiles and prepare the Inka's meals
ajotas/ajutas	traditional sandal today made from recycled tires
allin	literally, "good," part of a common Quechua greeting
alpaca	Andean camelid animal, hair used as weaving fiber
alqo yupi	a knitted design meaning "dog's paws"
altomisayoq	the highest level of Andean ritual specialist
anaku	Inca woman's dress, no longer used by Quechua women
Apu	Lord, as in nature spirits or local mountain gods
arpillera (S)	wall hanging made from scraps of cloth
ayahuasca	jungle vine prepared to induce hallucinogenic experiences
ayllu	groups joined by shared labor, lineage, social and/or land tenure relationships
ayni	reciprocal commitments for labor and goods, recompense in equal measure
bayeta/bayta (S)	coarsely woven sheep wool used for fabric
cabañuelas (S)	the act of predicting next year's weather from the beginning days of August
cargo (S)	method of sponsorship for community festivals, offices and obligations
carguyoq	one who accepts a cargo responsibility
chaki	literally, "foot," a design sometimes used in the textile trims
chakitajlla	an Andean foot plow
chaleco (S)	a vest-shaped garment
charki	sun-dried llama meat
chaska	literally "star," also a textile design
chicha	locally made fermented-corn beer
chili-chili	a medicinal plant often depicted in weavings
chiquira	handmade pre-Columbian beads
chiri	literally, "cold"
chiri wayra	refers to the cold winds frequently experienced at high altitudes
chollo (S)	a person of Quechua origins who learns Spanish and converts to a modern lifestyle

chullo	Quechua man's earflapped knitted hat
chuncho	ceremonial dance character mythically depicting inhabitants of the jungle
chunka	the number ten
chuño	freeze-dried potatoes
chuspa	a woven bag for carrying coca leaves
comparsas (S)	festival groups including dancers, sponsors, and all helpers
costales (S)	large storage and transport sacks
demanda (S)	carved wooden box with a photo of a patron saint or Jesus
despacho (S)	offerings by a misayoq to the mountain gods
hampeq	a healer or doctor
hanan pacha	the upper earth or world above, the afterlife
hatun	large or great
hoyona	a short waistcoat, often highly decorated
huasca	a weaving design depicting a particular lake shape
huatanay/watanay	
	a favorite plant used to season roasted guinea pig
huatia	an earthen oven made of dirt clods for baking potatoes
hurin pacha	lower earth or the underworld
hurka	community activity to solicit help for a cargo
ichu/ischu	tall native grasses of the puna
inti	sun
iskay	the number two
iskayoq	the number two with a suffix to indicate termination of a number sequence
kawsay	to exist, to live, life and health
kaypacha	this world we live in, the present world
kaypina	women's carrying cloth
kero	a drinking cup for ritual sharing of beverages
k'intu	a form for ritual exchange of coca
kiwicha	a high protein Andean grain
laut'a	a red-fringed head adornment worn only by the Inka
llama	large Andean camelid, a beast of burden
lliclla	woman's shoulder cloth
llipta	ash (lime) catalyst that activates the alkaloids in the coca leaf
majeno (S)	dance character inspired by Spanish influence
mama coca	the sacred mother coca leaf
mamacha	a form of greeting and endearment for a woman

mamaqocha	the mother lake, the ocean and Lake Titicaca
maqta	a primary character for the Chileno dance
misayoq	the various levels of Andean ritual specialists
montera (S)	a woman's head covering of several shapes
moraya	a form of dehydrated tuber
ñawi	literally, "eye," a design often used on the trim of textiles
ñawpa	ancient or old
oca	indigenous sweet tuber in several colors
ollas (S)	large cooking pots
pacha	Earth, world, age
pachacuti	a mythical time shift instituting a new world order
Pachamama	Mother Earth
pachamanka	an oven made of stones dug into the ground generally used to cook a whole sheep and potatoes for a festive occasion
pachaq chaki	literally, "one hundred feet," a type of woven bag used to carry coins and money
paco	the beginning misayoq, a trainee or initiate
pago	an offering to the mountain gods (despacho)
pallay	textile designs, literally "to pick up threads"
pampamisayoq	an Andean ritual specialist
paqarin	tomorrow, to emerge, place of origin
paqariy	to emerge, to found, to become morning
pauluchas	bear-like creatures
pichincho/pinchincho/pinchinqo	
	a small Andean bird often depicted in textiles
polleras (S)	indigenous skirts made of bayeta
puna	high-altitude regions with cold climates
puska/pushka	a distaff spindle for hand spinning yarn
puyto	the woven trim attached to polleras
qayto	textiles made entirely of natural materials
qenqo	zigzag, often symbolizes lightning or rivers
quipu	information coded on knotted strings
runakuna	the people, human beings, humankind
runasimi	the Quechua language
rutuy/rutuyku/rutuchikuy	
	the rite of passage called first haircutting
sanqapa	small woven bands for securely fastening hats
sasa	an action that is difficult or hard to do

sentillo	a man's hatband
sonqo	literally, "heart"
Tahuantinsuyo	original name for the Inca empire
tawa	literally, the number four
t'ika	literally, flower
tiyay	to inhabit a place, to reside within
tocapu	a series of design elements in Inca textiles
tupu	a pin for fastening textiles
ukuku	the bear character in ceremonial festivities
unku	Inca man's tunic, a shape still used by Q'eros
unkuna	a woven cloth for carrying coca and personal belongings
unkunita	a small cloth for protecting a ritual offering until it is ceremoniously burned
vicuña	the smallest Andean camelid with the softest and most highly prized hair
viscacha	an Andean rodent depicted in textile designs
warmi	woman
wawa	a baby
wawatusuchiy	a ritual sometimes practiced at weddings
wichuna	a llama bone pick for making woven designs
wincha	a woman's headband
wira	literally "fat," foam of the sea

APPENDIX
Ritual and Agricultural Cycle of Inca Culture

The annual agricultural and ritual cycle of the Incas with the individual month names as noted on the calendar were prepared by D. Manuel Chávez Ballón and the Department of Archaeology at the Universidad Nacional de San Antonio Abad in Cuzco. The monthly activities and related festivals derive from Garcilaso de la Vega ([1609] 1961) based on drawings of the religious cycle by Guamán (Huamán) Poma. Additional information is noted by source. Contemporary Catholic dates are cited after the Inca dates.

Inti Raymi (June). The Inka is represented drinking with the Sun at the Feast of Inti Raymi (now observed on June 24; from Vega). June 24 is San Juan feast day and June 28 is San Pedro feast day. Pentecost is followed by Qoyllur R'iti and Corpus Christi (movable feasts), and the end of the potato harvest.

Anta Sitwa (July). The harvest festival; the high priest making an agrarian sacrifice; storage of food, making chuño and charki. (Vega) The Virgin of Carmen feast days are observed on July 16–18. July 25 is the day of the animals ("animals' birthday"), and also St. Santiago's day. July 28 is Peruvian Independence Day (national).

Qhapaq Sitwa (August). The feast of tilling; four Incas are shown digging while a woman brings them chicha. (Vega) The month for agricultural predictions for the coming year by altomisayoqs and pampamisayoqs. Pagos are made to the earth for the thirst and hunger that the Pachamama is experiencing. First Inca day after the sun's nadir passage is August 18, which determined the first day of planting. (Zuidema 1990) August is the month that the Pachamama opens up. (Randall 1990:22)

Quya (Qoya) Raymi (September). Great feast of the Moon, wife of the Sun. The town of Cuzco is purified. (Vega) Planting month, the return of the female principle to the earth and fertility. The only month dedicated exclusively to women. (Zuidema 1990; Randall 1990) September 14–20 is the pilgrimage of El Señor de Huanca.

Uno(u) Raymi (October). Procession to ask God for water; the hungry black sheep (llama) helps men to weep and ask God for water. (Vega) Early rains are possible. *Unu* is Quechua for water. Planting is the major activity and continues in October.

Aya Marka (November). Feast of the Dead. The mummies of dead kings are carried in state. They are given food, clothed in rich robes with feathers on their heads; the people sing and dance in their company and carry them through the streets to the main square. (Vega) All Saints Day or All Souls Day, November 1–2. Beginning of the rainy season.

Qhapaq Raymi (December) Capac Inti Raimi. This is the great feast of the Sun, the king of the heavens, planets, and stars, and of all up above. Much gold and silver is sacrificed to the Sun, human sacrifices of young boys and girls, followed by a great feast. (Vega) Twelve days of Christmas, December 24–January 6.

Kamay (January). Inca penance and fasting, bodies covered with ashes, offering of sacrifices, and traveling in procession to the temples of the Sun and the Moon, their gods and all huacas. (Vega)

Hatun Puquy (February). The Inca made offerings of great quantities of gold and silver. The Inka is shown kneeling, bareheaded, making an offering. This is the wet season, and rains are frequent. Visits made to huacas of the high mountains and snows. (Vega) Carnival is a major Andean celebration with dancing for at least a full week.

Pacha Puquy (March). The Inka is represented kneeling, about to sacrifice a black sheep (llama). The priests performed many ceremonies, did not eat salt or fruit, and did not have contact with women. Catholics observe Lent and Easter.

Inka Raymi (April). Feast of the King. They sacrificed red sheep (llamas). A great feast to which all the lords, princes, and "poor" Incas were invited. They ate, sang, and danced on the main square (of Cuzco). (Vega) Corpus Christi, the Catholic movable feast replaced the fixed dates of the first helical rise of the Pleiades (Arriaga [1621] 1968:213) in early June, announcing the time and the direction of the June solstice. By Inca custom, kings of subject nations or their delegates presented themselves at the court in Cuzco during the dry season. (Zuidema 1990) It is a time for travel. The Pleiades disappear, and the female principle (and thus fertility) also goes underground. The male principle is dominant until August or Qoya Raymi. (Randall 1990) There was a great festival to honor the sun, along with great sadness because the sun had passed its nadir, the lowest point at sunset on April 26 until it returns on August 18. April 19–26 marked a great festival to give thanks and mourn the sun's departure. (Randall 1990:14)

Aymuray (May). The illustration shows Indians carrying supplies of potatoes to the warehouses. It was the feast of Aymnuray (Vega says "*aimara*," which could be mistaken for the Aymara people). Great drunkenness and singing. (Vega) May 3, Santa Cruz is observed as Cruz Velakuy or the two-night vigilance with the cross and the dressing of the cross. It is called the cargo of the crosses and is an actual cargo responsibility. The crosses are dressed, given new clothes, and candles are burned all night in front of them. Cruz Velakuy is not a movable feast. People dance indoors and visit particular crosses. The maize harvest has been collected and the potatoes still must be harvested. Thus, Cruz Velakuy is a celebration of the early harvest and maize preservation for the coming year. (Cobo 1990:41) "The harvest symbolized the separation of the male/female principles, when the female goes underground, to the ocean." (Randall 1990:35) It was the last celebration of the Inca calendar marking the end of the agricultural year.

Every year after the maize harvest, the aclla in Cuzco served a sumptuous banquet. The next day they presented the Inka with all the cloth they had woven during the year and the Inka admitted new aclla into the acllawasi (the house of the chosen women). (Randall 1990:13)

The continued use of the same agricultural and ritual dates indicates the continuity of observed practices over time. The cycle of agricultural rites to ensure crop fertility as well as abundant herds appears to continue today with an overlay of Spanish names of Catholic saints and holy days. The documents cited here provide evidence of the roots of some contemporary Quechua agricultural and ritual practices.

BIBLIOGRAPHY

Abrams, David. 1996. *The Spell of the Sensuous.* New York: Vintage Books.

Abu-Lughod, Lila. 1991. Writing Against Culture. In Richard G. Fox, ed., *Recapturing Anthropology: Working in the Present,* 137–62. Santa Fe, N.Mex.: School of American Research Press; distributed by University of Washington Press.

Adelson, Laurie, and Arthur Tracht. 1983. *Aymara Weavings: Textiles of Colonial and 19th-Century Bolivia.* Washington, D.C.: Smithsonian Institute Traveling Exhibition Service.

Allen, Catherine J. 1978. Private and Communal Rituals in a Quechua Village, Coca, Chicha and Trago. Ph.D. diss., University of Illinois, Champaign-Urbana.

———. 1983. Of Bear-Men and He-Men: Bear Metaphors and Male Self-Perception in a Peruvian Community. *Latin American Indian Literatures Journal* 7, no. 1: 38–51.

———. 1988. *The Hold Life Has: Coca and Cultural Identity in an Andean Community.* Washington, D.C.: Smithsonian Institution Press.

Amano, Yoshitaro. 1979. *Textiles of the Andes.* San Francisco: Heian International.

Amiotte, Arthur. 1992. The Call to Remember. *Parabola Magazine.* 17, no. 3: 34.

Arguedas, José María. 1978. *Deep Rivers.* Austin: University of Texas Press.

Arias Sanchez, Oscar. 2000. Chancellor's lecture series. Boone, N.C.: Appalachian State University, 17 October.

Arriaga, Pablo José de. [1621] 1968. *The Extirpation of Idolatry in Peru.* Trans. and ed. L. Clark Keating. Lexington: University Press of Kentucky.

Ascher, Marcia, and Robert Ascher. 1981. *Code of the Quipu: A Study in Media, Mathematics, and Culture.* Ann Arbor: University of Michigan Press.

Aveni, Anthony. 1992. Pre-Columbian Images of Time. In Richard F. Townsend, ed., *The Ancient Americas: Art from Sacred Landscapes,* 49–60. Chicago: Art Institute of Chicago; Munich: Prestel Verlag.

Babcock, Barbara. 1982. Clay Voices: Invoking, Mocking, Celebrating. In Victor Turner, ed., *Celebration: Studies in Festivity and Ritual,* 58–76. Washington, D.C.: Smithsonian Institution Press.

Barnes, Ruth, and Joanne B. Eicher. 1992. *Dress and Gender: Making and Meaning in Cultural Contexts.* New York: Berg; distributed by St. Martin's Press.

Basso, Keith H., and Henry A. Selby, eds. 1976. *Meaning in Anthropology.* Albuquerque: University of New Mexico Press.

Bastien, Joseph W. 1978. *Mountain of the Condor: Metaphor and Ritual in an Andean Ayllu.* St. Paul, Minn.: West Publishing.

Bawden, Garth. 1996. *The Moche.* Cambridge, Mass.: Blackwell.

Bean, Susan. 1994. The Fabric of Independence. *Parabola* 19, no. 3: 29–42.

Bennett, Hal Zina. 1994. From the Heart of the Andes: An Interview with Americo Yabar. *Shaman's Drum* 36, Fall: 40–49.

Bennett, Wendell Clark, and Junius B. Bird. 1949. *Andean Culture History.* New York: American Museum of Natural History.

Bills, Garland D., Bernardo Vallejo C., and Rudolph C. Troike. 1969. *An Introduction to Spoken Bolivian Quechua.* Austin: University of Texas Press.

Bird, Junius B. 1954. *Paracas Fabrics and Nazca Needlework, 3d Century B.C.–3rd Century a.d.* Technical analysis by Louisa Bellinger. Washington, D.C.: National Publishing Company.

Boone, Elizabeth Hill, ed. 1996. *Andean Art at Dumbarton Oaks.* 2 vols. Washington, D.C.: Dumbarton Oaks Research Library and Collection.

Boone, Elizabeth Hill, and Walter J. Mignolo, eds. 1994. *Writing without Words: Alternative Literacies in Mesoamerica and the Andes.* Durham, N.C.: Duke University Press.

Braun, Barbara. 1995. *Arts of the Amazon.* London: Thames and Hudson.

Brinckerhoff, Deborah. 1999. *Weaving for the Gods: Textiles of the Ancient Andes.* Greenwich, Conn.: Bruce Museum.

Bruner, Edward. 1986. Ethnography as Narrative. In Victor Turner and Edward Bruner, eds., *The Anthropology of Experience,* 139–58. Chicago: University of Illinois Press.

Carpenter, Lawrence. 1992. Inside-Out, Which Side Counts? In Robert V. H. Dover, Katherine E. Seibold, and John H. McDowell, eds., *Andean Cosmologies Through Time: Persistence and Emergence,* 115–36. Bloomington: University of Indiana Press.

Cereceda, Veronica. 1986. The Semiology of Andean Textiles: The Talegas of Isluga. In John V. Murra, Nathan Watchel, and Jacques Revel, eds., *Anthropological History of Andean Polities,* 149–73. New York: Cambridge University Press; Paris: Editions de la Maison des sciences de l'homme.

Chicago, Judy. 2001. Interview. National Public Radio, aired by KUNM, Albuquerque, New Mexico, 27 July.

Chino, Conroy, et al. *Surviving Columbus.* 1992. Produced by KNME/Albuquerque and Institute of American Indian Arts. 120 min. Alexandria, Va.: PBS Video. Videocassette.

Classen, Constance. 1993a. *Inca Cosmology and the Human Body.* Salt Lake City: University of Utah Press.

——————. 1993b. *Worlds of Sense: Exploring the Senses in History and Across Cultures.* London and New York: Routledge Press.

Clifford, James. 1988. *The Predicament of Culture.* Cambridge: Harvard University Press.

Clifford, James, and George E. Marcus. 1986. *Writing Culture: The Poetics and Politics of Ethnography.* Berkeley: University of California Press.

Cobo, Bernabé. 1983. *History of the Inca Empire.* Trans. and ed. by Roland Hamilton. Austin: University of Texas Press.

——————. 1990. *Inca Religion and Customs.* Trans. and ed. by Roland Hamilton. Austin: University of Texas Press.

Collier, John Jr., and Malcolm Collier. 1986. *Visual Anthropology: Photography as a Research Method*. Albuquerque: University of New Mexico Press.

Conklin, William J. 1996. Structure as Meaning in Ancient Andean Textiles. In *Andean Art at Dumbarton Oaks,* Vol. 2, 321–28. Washington, D.C.: Dumbarton Oaks Research Library and Collection.

Crumrine, N. R., and M. Halpin. 1983. *The Power of Symbols: Masks and Masquerade in the Americas*. Vancouver: University of British Columbia Press.

Cummins, Tom. 1994. Representation in the Sixteenth Century and the Colonial Image of the Inca. In Elizabeth Hill Boone, and Walter J. Mignolo, eds., *Writing without Words: Alternative Literacies in Mesoamerica and the Andes,* 188–219. Durham, N.C.: Duke University Press.

D'Azevedo, Warren L. 1958. A Structural Approach to Aesthetics: Toward a Definition of Art in Anthropology. *American Anthropologist* 60: 702–14.

Demarest, A. Viracocha. 1981. *The Nature and Antiquity of the Andean High God*. Monograph 9. Cambridge: Peabody Museum.

Donnan, Christopher B. 1978. *Moche Art of Peru: Pre-Columbian Symbolic Communication*. Rev. ed. Los Angeles: Museum of Cultural History, University of California.

Dover, Robert V. H., Katherine H. Seibold, and John H. McDowell, eds. 1992. *Andean Cosmologies Through Time: Persistence and Emergence*. Bloomington: Indiana University Press.

Durkheim, Emile. [1915] 1954. *The Elementary Forms of Religious Life*. New York: Free Press.

Emery, Irene, and Patricia Fiske, eds. 1977. *Ethnographic Textiles of the Western Hemisphere*. Washington, D.C.: Textile Museum.

Erdoes, Richard, and Alfonso Ortiz. 1984. *American Indian Myths and Legends*. New York: Pantheon Books.

Ereira, Alan, et al. 1991. *From the Heart of the World*. Produced by British Broadcasting Company. 110 minutes. New York: Mystic Fire Video. Videocassette.

Femenias, Blenda, with Mary Ann Medlin, Lynn Meisch, and Elayne Zorn. 1987. *Andean Aesthetics: Textiles of Peru and Bolivia*. Madison: University of Wisconsin Press.

Fisher, Michael M. J. 1986. Ethnicity and the Post-Modern Arts. In James Clifford and George Marcus, eds., *Writing Culture: The Poetics and Politics of Ethnography,* 194–233. Berkeley: University of California Press.

Flores Ochoa, Jorge. 1968. *Pastoralists of the Andes: The Alpaca Herders of Paratía*. Philadelphia: Institute for the Study of Human Issues.

————. 1986. The Classification and Naming of South American Camelids. In John V. Murra, Nathan Watchel, and Jacques Revel, eds., *Anthropological History of Andean Polities*. New York: Cambridge University Press; Paris: Editions de la Maison des sciences de l'homme.

Flores Ochoa, J., and A. M. Fries. 1989. *Puna, Qheswa, Yunga: El Hombre y Su Medio en Q'ero*. Lima: Banco Central de Reserva del Peru, Collecciones Andinas.

Fox, Richard G. 1991 Introduction. In Richard G. Fox, ed., *Recapturing Anthropology: Working in the Present,* 1–16. Santa Fe: School of American Research Press;

distributed by University of Washington Press.

Frame, Mary. 1986. The Visual Images of Fabric Structures in Ancient Peruvian Art. In Ann P. Rowe, ed., *The Junius B. Bird Conference on Andean Textiles,* 47–80. Washington, D.C.: Textile Museum.

——————. 1991. Structure, Image and Abstractions: Paracas Necropolis Headbands as System Templates. In Anne Paul, ed., *Paracas Art and Architecture: Object and Context in South Coastal Peru,* 110–71. Iowa City: University of Iowa Press.

Gayton, Ann H. 1961. The Cultural significance of Peruvian Textiles: Production, Function, Aesthetics. *Kroeber Anthropological Society Papers* 25: 111–28.

——————. 1973. The Cultural Significance of Peruvian Textiles. In J. H. Rowe and D. Menzel, eds., *Peruvian Archaeology,* 275–92. Palo Alto, Calif.: Peek Publishers.

Geertz, Clifford. 1973. *The Interpretation of Cultures.* New York: Basic Books.

——————. 1976. Art as a Cultural System. *MLN* (Modern Language Notes) 91: 1473–99.

González Holguín, Diego. [1608] 1952. *Vocabulario de la lengua general de todo el Perú llamada lengua qquichua o del Inca.* Lima: Imprenta Santa María.

Gow, David D. 1976. The Gods and Social Change in the High Andes. Ph.D. diss., University of Wisconsin, Madison.

Graburn, Nelson H. H. 1976. *Ethnic and Tourist Arts: Cultural Expressions from the Fourth World.* Berkeley: University of California Press.

Gravelle Lecount, Cynthia. 1990. *Andean Folk Knitting, Traditions and Techniques from Peru and Bolivia.* St. Paul, Minn.: Dos Tejadoras Press.

Green, Duncan. 1997. *Faces of Latin America.* London: Latin American Bureau.

Guamán Poma de Ayala, Felipe. 1980. *Primer nueva coronica y buen gobierno.* Mexico: Siglo Veintiuno.

Harrison, Regina. 1989. *Signs, Songs and Memory in the Andes.* Austin: University of Texas Press.

Heckman, Andrea M. 1997. Quechua Cultural Continuity and Change as Reflected by the Traditional Textiles of Ausangate, Peru. Ph.D. diss., University of New Mexico, Albuquerque.

Hill, Jonathan D., ed. 1988. *Rethinking History and Myth: Indigenous South American Perspectives on the Past.* Urbana: University of Illinois Press.

Hyslop, John. 1990. *Inca Settlement Planning.* Austin: University of Texas Press.

Kahlenberg, Mary Hunt, ed. 1998. *The Extraordinary in the Ordinary.* New York: Harry Abrams in association with the Museum of International Folk Art, Museum of New Mexico.

Karp, Ivan, and Steven D. Lavine, eds. 1991. *Exhibiting Cultures: The Poetics and Politics of Museum Display.* Washington, D.C.: Smithsonian Institution Press.

Lavalle, José Antonio de, and Rosario de Lavalle de Cárdenas, eds. 1999. *Tejidos Milenarios.* Lima: Integra AFP.

Locke, L. Leland. 1923. *The Ancient Quipu or Peruvian Knot Record.* New York: American Museum of Natural History.

Lumbreras, Luis G. 1974. *The Peoples and Cultures of Ancient Peru.* Trans. Betty J. Meggers. Washington, D.C.: Smithsonian Institution Press.

Lynch, Thomas F., ed. 1980. *Guitarrero Cave: Early Man in the Andes.* New York: Academic Press.

Lyon, Patricia J., ed. 1974. *Native South Americans: Ethnology of the Least Known Continent.* Prospect Heights, Ill.: Waveland Press.

MacCormick, Sabine. 1991. *Religion in the Andes.* Princeton, N.J.: Princeton University Press.

Mails, Thomas E. 1991. *Fools Crow: Wisdom and Power.* Norman: Oklahoma University Press.

Maquet, Jacques Jérôme. 1971. *Introduction to Aesthetic Anthropology.* Reading, Mass.: Addison-Wesley.

Marcus, George E., and Michael M. J. Fisher. 1986. *Anthropology as Cultural Critique.* Chicago: University of Chicago Press.

Mauss, Marcel. 1990. *The Gift.* New York: W. W. Norton.

Meisch, Lynn A. 1987. The Living Textiles of Tarabuco, Bolivia. In Blenda Femenias, ed., *Andean Aesthetics: Textiles of Peru and Bolivia,* 46–59. Madison: University of Wisconsin Press.

—————, ed. 1997. *Traditional Textiles of the Andes.* London: Thames and Hudson.

Messenger, Phyllis M., ed. 1991. *The Ethics of Collecting Cultural Property.* Albuquerque: University of New Mexico Press.

Meyerson, Julia. 1990. *'Tambo, Life in an Andean Village.* Austin: University of Texas Press.

Montufar M., Uriel. 1991. *Diccionario Quechua-Español; Español-Quechua.* Arequipa, Peru: Author.

Morató Peña, Luis. 1981. *Quechua Boliviano.* Cochabamba, Bolivia: Instituto de Idiomas "Tawantinsuyu."

—————. 1997. Quechua Diccionario. Ithaca, N.Y.: Cornell University. Photocopy.

Moseley, Michael E. 1992. *The Incas and Their Ancestors.* London: Thames and Hudson.

Morris, Craig. 1986. Storage, Supply and Redistribution in the Economy of the Inca State. In John V. Murra, Nathan Watchel, and Jacques Revel, eds., *Anthropological History of Andean Polities.* New York: Cambridge University Press; Paris: Editions de la Maison des sciences de l'homme.

Murra, John V. 1962. Cloth and Its Functions in the Inca State. *American Anthropologist* 64, no. 4: 710–27.

—————. 1972. El "control vertical" de un máximo de pesos ecologicos en la economía de las sociedades andinas. In Iñigo Ortiz de Zúñiga, Visita de la Provincia de Leon de Huánuco en 1562, Iñigo Ortiz de Zúñiga, Visitador. Huánuco, Peru: Universidad Nacional Hemilio Valdizán, Facultad de Letras y Educación.

—————. 1978. Introduction. In José María Arguedas, *Deep Rivers,* ix–xv. Austin: University of Texas Press.

—————. 1980a. *The Economic Organization of the Inka State.* Greenwich, Conn.: JAI Press.

—————————. 1980b. *Incas.* Public Broadcasting Associates, PBS and the Pacific Arts. Los Angeles: Nesmith Enterprises. 58 minutes. Videocassette.

Murra, John V., Nathan Watchel, and Jacques Revel, eds. 1986. *Anthropological History of Andean Polities.* New York: Cambridge University Press; Paris: Editions de la Maison des sciences de l'homme.

Neruda, Pablo. 1985. *Windows that Open Inward: Images of Chile.* New York: White Swan Press.

Núñez del Prado B., Juan Victor. 1974. The Supernatural World of the Quechua of Southern Peru as Seen from the Community of Qotobamba. In Patricia J. Lyon, ed., *Native South Americans,* 238–50. Prospect Hills: Waveland Press.

Núñez del Prado, Juan, and L. J. Murillo. 1996. Preparando un Inca. *Crónicas Urbanas* Spring: 115–22.

Núñez del Prado, Oscar. 1973. *Kuyo Chico: Applied Anthropology in an Indian Community.* Trans. Lucy Whyte Russo and Richard Russo. Chicago: University of Chicago Press.

O'Neal, Lila. 1949. Weaving. In Julian Haynes Steward, ed., *Handbook of South American Indians,* prepared in cooperation with the United States Department of State as a project of the Interdepartmental Committee on Cultural and Scientific Cooperation, Vol. 5, 121–37. Washington, D.C.: Government Printing Office.

Ortiz, Alfonso. 1969. *The Tewa World: Space, Time, Being and Becoming in a Pueblo Society.* Chicago: University of Chicago Press.

—————————. 1994. The Dynamics of Pueblo Cultural Survival. In Raymond J. Demallie and Alfonso Ortiz, eds., *North American Indian Anthropology,* 296–306. Norman: University of Oklahoma Press.

Paul, Anne. 1990. *Paracas Ritual Attire: Symbols of Authority in Ancient Peru.* Norman: University of Oklahoma Press.

Paz, Octavio. 1974. Use and Contemplation. Essay, in Paz, *In Praise of Hands: Contemporary Crafts of the World.* Greenwich, Conn.: New York Graphic Society.

Peters, Ann. 1991. Ecology and Society in Embroidered Images from the Paracas Necropolis. In Anne Paul, ed., *Paracas Art and Architecture: Object and Context in South Coastal Peru,* 240–314. Iowa City: University of Iowa Press.

Poole, Deborah Ann. 1984. Ritual-Economic Calendars in Paruro: The Structure of Representation in Andean Ethnography. Ph.D. diss., University of Illinois, Champaign-Urbana.

Pratt, Mary Louise. 1999. Apocalypse in the Andes. *Americas Magazine* 51, no. 4: 38–47.

Quinn, Daniel. 1996. *The Story of B.* New York: Bantam Books.

Radner, Joan Newlon. 1993. *Feminist Messages: Coding in Women's Folk Culture.* Urbana: University of Illinois Press.

Randall, Robert. 1982. Qoyllur Rit'i, An Inca Fiesta of the Pleiades: Reflections on Time and Space in the Andean World. *Boletín del Instituto Francés de Estudios Andinos* (Lima) 11, nos. 1–2: 37–81.

—————————. 1987a. Return of the Pleiades. *Natural History* 96, no. 6.

—————————. 1987b. Del tiempo y del rio. *Boletín de Lima* 54, November: 69–95.

—————————. 1990. The Mythstory of Kuri Qoyllur. *Journal of Latin American Lore* 16, no. 1: 3–45.

Redfield, Robert. 1941. *Folk Culture of the Yucatán*. Chicago: University of Chicago Press.

──────. 1956. *Peasant Society and Culture: An Anthropological Approach to Civilization*. Chicago: University of Chicago Press.

Reeve, Mary-Elizabeth. 1988. *Los Quichua del Curaray: El Proceso de Formación de la Identidad*. Trans. Maria del Carmen Andrade. Guayaquil: Museo, Banco Central del Ecuador; Quito, Ecuador: Ediciones ABYA-YALA.

Reid, James W. 1986. *Textile Masterpieces of Ancient Peru*. New York: Dover Publications.

──────. 1989. *The Textile Art of Peru*. Edited by J. A. Gonzalo Lavalle and J. A. Garcia. *The Textile Art of Peru*. Lima: Industria Textil Piura.

Roe, Peter G. 1993. Marginal Men: Male Artists among the Shipibo Indians of Peru. In Richard L. Anderson and Karen L. Field, eds., *Art in Small-Scale Societies: Contemporary Readings,* 247–66. Englewood Cliffs, N.J.: Prentice-Hall.

Rowe, Ann Pollard. 1977a. Weaving Styles in the Cuzco Area. In Irene Emery and Patricia Fiske, eds., *Ethnographic Textiles of the Western Hemisphere: Irene Emery Roundtable on Museum Textiles, 1976 Proceedings,* 61–84. Washington, D.C.: Textile Museum.

──────. 1977b. *Warp-Patterned Weaves of the Andes*. Washington, D.C.: Textile Museum.

──────, ed. 1986. *The Junius B. Bird Conference on Andean Textiles, April 7th and 8th, 1984*. Washington, D.C.: Textile Museum.

──────, ed. 1998. *Costume and Identity in Highland Ecuador*. Text by Lynn A. Meisch, Laura M. Miller, Ann P. Rowe, et al. Washington, D.C.: Textile Museum.

Rowe, Ann Pollard and John Cohen. 2002. *Hidden Threads of Peru: Q'ero Textiles*. The Textile Museum, Washington, D.C. and Merrell Publishers, London.

Rowe, John H. 1946. Inca Culture at the Time of the Spanish Conquest. *The Bulletin of American Ethnology,* Vol. 2. Washington, D.C.: Smithsonian Institution, Bureau of American Ethnology.

──────. 1957. The Incas under Spanish Colonial Institutions. *Hispanic American Historical Review* 37: 155–99.

Rowe, John H. 1967a. An Interpretation of Radiocarbon Measurements on Archaeological Samples from Peru. In John H. Rowe and Dorothy Menzel, eds., *Peruvian Archaeology: Selected Readings,* 16–30. Palo Alto, Calif.: Peek Publications.

──────. 1967b. Colonial Portraits of Inca Nobles. In Sol Tax, ed., *The Civilizations of Ancient America: Selected Papers of the XXIXth International Congress of Americanists.* New York: Coopers Square Publishers.

──────. 1979. Standardization in Inca Tapestry Tunics. In Ann Pollard Rowe, Elizabeth P. Benson, and Anne-Louise Schaffer, eds., *The Junius B. Bird Pre-Columbian Textile Conference, May 19th and 20th, 1973,* 239–64. Washington, D.C.: Textile Museum.

Sallnow, Michael J. 1987. *Pilgrims of the Andes: Regional Cults in Cusco*. Washington, D.C.: Smithsonian Institution Press.

Salvador, Mari Lyn. 1978. *Yer Dailege! Kuna Women's Art*. Albuquerque: Maxwell Museum of Anthropology, University of New Mexico.

Sawyer, Alan R. 1961. Paracas and Nazca Iconography. In Samuel K. Lothrop, et al., *Essays in Pre-Columbian Art and Archaeology*, 393–406. Cambridge, Mass.: Harvard University Press.

————. 1963. Tiahuanaco Tapestry Designs. *Textile Museum Journal* 1, no. 2: 27–38.

Schevill, Margot Blum. 1986. *Costume as Communication: Ethnographic Costumes and Textiles from Middle America and the Central Andes of South America in the Collections of the Haffenreffer Museum of Anthropology, Brown University, Bristol, Rhode Island*. Bristol, R.I.: The Museum.

————. 1993. *Maya Textiles of Guatemala: The Gustavus A. Eisen Collection, 1902, the Hearst Museum of Anthropology, the University of California at Berkeley*. Austin: University of Texas Press.

Schevill, Margot Blum, Janet Catherine Berlo, and Edward B. Dwyer, eds. 1991. *Textile Traditions of Mesoamerica and the Andes: An Anthology*. New York: Garland.

Schwarz, Ronald A. 1979. Uncovering the Secret Vice: Toward Anthropology of Clothing and Adornment. In Justine Cordwell and Ronald A. Schwarz, eds., *The Fabrics of Culture: The Anthropology of Clothing and Adornment*, 23–45. The Hague; New York: Moulton.

Seibold, Katharine E. 1992. Textiles and Cosmology in Choquecancha, Cuzco, Peru. In Robert V. H. Dover, Katharine E. Seibold, and John H. McDowell, eds., *Andean Cosmologies Through Time: Persistence and Emergence*, 166–201. Bloomington: Indiana University Press.

Sherbondy, Jeanette E. 1992. Water Ideology in Inca Ethnogenesis. In Robert V. H. Dover, Katharine E. Seibold, and John H. McDowell, eds., *Andean Cosmologies Through Time: Persistence and Emergence*. Bloomington: University of Indiana Press.

Silverman, Gail P. 1999. Cuzco and Its Relation to Inca Tocapu. In José Antonio de Lavalle and Rosario de Lavalle de Cárdenas, eds., *Tejidos Milenarios*, 803–36. Lima: Integra AFP.

Silverman-Proust, Gail P. 1988. Weaving Technique and the Registration of Knowledge in the Cuzco Area of Peru. *Journal of Latin American Lore* 14, no. 2: 207–41.

Spalding, Karen. 1984. *Huarochiri: An Andean Society under Inca and Spanish Rule*. Palo Alto, Calif.: Stanford University Press.

Stephan, Ruth W. 1957. Collected by José María Arguedas and others. *The Singing Mountaineers: Songs and Tales of the Quechua People*. Austin: University of Texas Press.

Stocking, George, ed. 1985. *Objects and Others: Essays on Museum and Material Culture*. Madison: University of Wisconsin Press.

Stone-Miller, Rebecca. 1992a. *To Weave for the Sun: Ancient Andean Textiles*. London: Thames and Hudson.

————. 1992b. Camelids and Chaos in Huari and Tiwanaku Textiles. In Richard F. Townsend, ed., *The Ancient Americas: Art from Sacred Landscapes*, 335–46. Chicago: Art Institute of Chicago; Munich: Prestel Verlag.

Tedlock, Dennis. 1983. *The Spoken Word and the Work of Interpretation*. Philadelphia: University of Pennsylvania Press.

Townsend, Richard F., ed. 1992. *The Ancient Americas: Art from Sacred Landscapes.* Chicago: Art Institute of Chicago; Munich: Prestel Verlag.

Turner, Victor. 1969. *The Ritual Process.* Chicago: Aldine.

——————. 1974. *Dramas, Fields, and Metaphors: Symbolic Action in Human Society.* Ithaca, N.Y.: Cornell University Press.

Turner, Victor, and Edward M. Bruner. 1986. *The Anthropology of Experience.* Urbana: University of Illinois Press.

Turner, Victor, and Edith Turner. 1978. *Image and Pilgrimage in Christian Culture: Anthropological Perspectives.* New York: Columbia University Press.

Urton, Gary. 1985. *Animal Myths and Metaphors in South America.* Salt Lake City: University of Utah Press.

——————. 1988. *At the Crossroads of the Earth and the Sky: An Andean Cosmology.* Austin: University of Texas Press.

Valcárcel, Carlos D. 1970. *Túpac Amaru: El Revolucionario.* Lima: Moncloa-Campodonico Editores.

Van Maanen, John. 1988. *Tales of the Field: On Writing Ethnography.* Chicago: University of Chicago Press.

Vega, Garcilaso de la. [1609] 1961. *Royal Commentaries of the Incas, and General History of Peru.* N.p.: Orion Press.

Wade, Edwin, and Evans, David. 1973. The Kachina Sash: A Native Model of the Hopi World. *Western Folklore* 32, no. 1: 1–18.

Weiner, Annette B., and Jane Schneider. 1991. *Cloth and Human Experience.* Washington, D.C.: Smithsonian Institution Press.

Wilson, Monica. 1954. Nyakyusa Ritual and Symbolism. *American Anthropologist* 56, no 2: 241.

Wright, Ronald, with Nilda Callañaupa. 1989. *Quechua Phrasebook.* Hawthorn, Vic., Australia; Berkeley, Calif.: Lonely Planet.

Zorn, Elayne. 1987. Encircling Meaning: Economics and Aesthetics in Taquile, Peru. In Blenda Femenias, ed., *Andean Aesthetics: Textiles of Peru and Bolivia,* 67–79. Madison: University of Wisconsin Press.

Zuidema, R. Tom. 1981. Inca Observations of the Solar and Lunar Passages Through Zenith and Anti-Zenith at Cuzco. In Ray A. Williamson, ed., *Archaeoastronomy in the New World,* 319–42. Los Altos, Calif.: Ballena Press.

——————. 1983. Masks in the Incaic Solstice and Equinoctial Rituals. In N. R. Crumrine and M. Halpin, eds., *The Power of Symbols,* 146–53. Vancouver: University of British Columbia Press.

——————. 1990. *Inca Civilization in Cuzco.* Austin: University of Texas Press.

INDEX